To Clifford.   14·2·08 .

Hope you enjoy this
as much as I have.

          John + Audrey.

HAPPY BIRTHDAY.

John Pepper's COMPLETE Norn Iron Haunbook

"Fower John Pepper Volumes in Wan"

Ulster-English Dictionary

Ulster Phrasebook

Illustrated Encyclopedia of Ulster Knowledge

Ulster Haunbook

Appletree Press

For Bettie, in acknowledgement of the helpfulness of a wife able to accept without a grumble the persistent pounding of a typewriter – just one of the tribulations built into life with an author

First published in 2004 by
Appletree Press Ltd
The Old Potato Station
14 Howard Street South
Belfast BT7 1AP

Tel: +44 (0) 28 90 24 30 74
Fax: +44 (0) 28 90 24 67 56
Web site: www.appletree.ie
Email: reception@appletree.ie

Editor: Jean Brown
Designer: Stuart Wilkinson
Production Manager: Paul McAvoy

John Pepper's Ulster-English Dictionary First published in 1981 by Appletree Press Ltd.

John Pepper's Ulster Phrasebook First published in 1983 by Appletree Press Ltd.

John Pepper's Illustrated Encyclopedia of Ulster Knowledge
First published in 1983 by Appletree Press Ltd.

John Pepper's Ulster Haunbook First published in 1987 by Appletree Press Ltd.

A catalogue record for this book is available from the British Library.

John Pepper's Complete Norn Iron Haunbook

ISBN-13: 978-0-86281-913-2

9 8 7 6 5 4 3 2

AP4054

Contents

Foreword

by Billy Simpson

In a world where language changes, adapts and renews itself with new manners of speech to suit the age or the fashion, a great deal of what makes our talk so colourful may be disappearing. If that decline has slowed a little in the last few decades it may have been because John Pepper taught us that our Ulsterisims were something to delight in and not be ashamed of. The cold electronic soul of the word processor cannot give birth to a description like 'He has a quare mouth for coolin' soup'. Or understand that impeccable logic of an Ulsterwoman who says, 'It was a lovely dress. It would have fitted me if I could have got it on.'

The Pepper column in *Belfast Telegraph*, which ran for almost thirty years, and the resulting books provided a window to a rich heritage of colourful language that defies category and most of the rules. Their author, Fred J. Gamble, had a gift for capturing and recording our conscious and unconscious humour 'It'll not take me long puttin' in an hour'), our malapropisms ('The army threw an accordian around the area'), our spoken shorthand that can condense an entire sentence enquiring whether or not a companion has had his lunch into just one short, sharp sound, 'Jeet?', or for the verbose, 'Jeet yit?'

All of us have heard these and other Ulsterisms, but until Pepper set them down in print for us we hardly realised they were there. Or that they were special and part of our quality as individuals in a world where individuality is being ironed out into a kind of trans-Atlantic computer-speak. In his own way John Pepper rescued some of that individuality for us in a way that touched the heart as well as the funnybone.

For Ulster exiles around the worlds, his books have become a touch of home, to be read and reread to evoke old memories and perhaps warm a wary spirit on a dark day.

He did not live to complete his work on the *Ulster Haunbook*, his final book, and it is shorter than originally planned. But there is much to enjoy in it and all the other books in this collection. All his books were illustrated by the brilliant drawings of Rowel Friers and Ralph Dobson. The John Pepper column was unique. The man who created and sustained it for nearly three decades was irreplaceable.

John Pepper's

Ulster-English Dictionary

Illustrated by
Rowel Friers

abitchary, death notice, assessment of some deceased: 'They had a whole abitchary of him in the paper.' 'The abitchary said he had a wide circle of frens. A wonder where they come from?'

achanee, expression of regret, longing, disappointment: 'Achanee but my heart's broke so it is.' 'Achanee but the trouble comes thick and fast.' 'Achanee, my heart's scalded.'

acit, indication of finality: 'Acit as far as I'm concerned.' 'Acit, I told him. I'm not going till say anor word.'

ack, expression of frustration, impatience, annoyance: 'Ack I know the woman well, but I can't mine her name.' 'Ack I forgot to mine it.' 'Ack it's been a shackin day.'

ackay, statement of confirmation or agreement: 'Ackay, I got the job done ages ago.' 'Ackay, she's not a bad wee girl.'

afeard, timid, alarmed, scared: 'She's afeard of her own skin.' 'He always says he's afeard of nathin but don't you believe it.'

affis bap, descriptive of person whose mental capacity is in doubt: 'The fella's affis bap.' 'Everybody knew the referee was affis bap.' See **buckijit**.

aganny, extreme pain or distress: 'I'm in aganny with my chilblains.' 'The big pixture was a load of oul rubbitch. I was in aganny luckin at it.'

11

agatalaff, indicates that the speaker was highly amused: 'She's a rare turn. Agatalaff ivvery time I'm in her house.' 'He's a comedian, the same boy. Agatalaff when I meet him.'

agayon, once more, repetition: 'Do ahafta ast ye agayon.' 'Tell you what, Jimmy. I'll hev the same agayon.' 'I'm sick, sore and tired of him. He was rightly agayon last night. As full as the Boyne.'

ahafta, faced with no alternative: 'Ahafta go ni. It's late.' 'Ahafta speak till her about the way she's gettin on.' 'Ahafta make up my mine about it.'

a hinnae onny, indicates that stocks are sold out, that supplies are finished; 'A hinnae onny sex' in Ballymena means that the speaker's supply of potato sacks is exhausted: 'I'd lenn ye all the tay ye want onny a hannae onny.' 'Just nivver ignore her. She hannae onny sense.'

ahint, behind, immediately to the rear: 'She was stannin ahint him.' 'Keep ahint me, chile, or ye'll get yerself lost, and then where wud ye be?'

aleckadoo, club official, usually of a rugby club; committee member, often considered out of touch with reality, generally envied because he never has to pay for admission: 'Once the aleckadoos lay down the law there's nothing anybody can do.' 'The stand was full of aleckadoos.'

allabess, expression of friendship and goodwill on parting: 'Allabess, Jimmy. Seeya soon.' 'Cheerio fer ni. Allabess.'

amawayon, announces the completion of a visit, the resumption of a journey; to go home: 'Amawayon back to the house.' See **amferaff.**

amblence, specially-equipped vehicle for carrying patients to hospital: 'They tuck him away in the amblence.' 'I knew there was somethin up when I saw the amblence sittin at her dure.'

amferaff, announcement of impending departure: 'Nightall. Amferaff.' 'It's been a long day. Amferaff ni.' 'That was a great night. Great. Amferaff.'

amferbedni, indicates impending retirement for the night: 'Cheerio then. Amferbedni.' 'Amferbedni. Cud ye give me a glassa water in a cup? 'Amferbedni. Ahafta be up at the scrake av dawn.'

am gie fu, 1. indicates that the speaker's appetite has been fully satisfied: 'That was a right fry I got. Am gie fu and that's a fact.' 2. an admission of intoxication: 'Shee me? Am gie fu.'

ammastannininyerlite, seeks an assurance that the speaker is not obstructing another's view of a window display, procession, exhibition, etc: 'Ammastannininyerlite? If I am, I'll move over.'

amoany coddin, explains that the speaker doesn't want to be taken seriously: 'Don't go losin yir bap. Sure amoany coddin.' 'Ye know rightly amoany coddin. Can't ye take a joke?'

annahydion, ignorant, ill-informed person: 'I can't stand him. He's nathin but an annahydion.'

anol, all the extras, all that goes with a particular set of circumstances: 'He has a wee car anol.' 'They have a bungalow with a garden anol.' 'That wee girl has a fine leg anol.'

arcan, diminutive person or creature, midget: 'He was jumpin about like an arcan.'

Armay, refers to the speaker's daughter, May; can also refer to a sister or an aunt: 'Armay's a great wee dancer.' 'Armay's a quare wee scholar.' 'Armay gat three ayes anna no at her exams.'

arrwuns, members of our family, relations: 'Arrwuns is goin till Spain for wor holidays.' 'Arrwuns always go till Millisle.' 'Arrwuns wud give anything for a good fry.'

ashy pot, lover of the fireside, someone constantly cold: 'She's a desperate ashy pot. Always huggin the fire.' 'My oul woman's turned into a right ashy pot.'

assay, denotes that the hearer's attention is being sought, a call to listen: 'Assay there, wait till ye hear this.' 'Assay, Joe. Wud ye lissen to me a minnit?' 'Assay there. Wud ye catch yirself on?'

assee leff, inquiry seeking to establish if someone has gone home: 'Assee leff yit? It's about time he tuk hisself aff.' 'I've been luckin everywhere for him. Asse leff?'

ast, request, seek a favour, make an enquiry: 'Clare, t'migod he ast me to marry him.' 'I ast him a civil question but 1 didden get a civil answer.' 'All ye hev to do is to ast and ye know ye won't get it.'

aster, to make a request, to question a female: 'The onny way to fine out is to aster.' 'I aster point blank but she wudden open her bake.' 'Twice I aster and six times she said no.'

ate-the-bolts, describes someone who is a glutton for activity, a work-aholic: 'That fella's a terrible ate-the-bolts.' 'See my oul woman? She fancies she married an ate-the-bolts. She huz anor think cummin.'

atterself, indicative of state of health: 'I knew the minnit she stepped across the dure she wasn't atterself.' 'That holiday did her a power of good. Ye cud see she's atterself again.'

aught, anything, nothing: 'I'm not well. I cannae dae aught in the house.' 'A cannae dae aught fer a hennae aught t'dae aught with.'

awa, indicates uncertainty, lapse of memory: 'I was talkin to awa last night. Y' know who I mean. The wee low set man with a stoop.' 'Did ye hear Awa on the television last night? Y' know? Thundergub.' 'I met Mrs Awa. She lives on the Ormo Road. The wumman that loves bakin tatey bread because it keeps her nails clean.'

awantin, sought for, needed urgently: 'Tell the wee girl she's awantin.' 'Me? Sure I'm always awantin. M'ma won't let me outav her sight.'

awayerthon, indicates disbelief, warns that the speaker is aware that his or her leg is being pulled; Ulster version of 'Tell that to the marines': 'Awayerthon, woman. I wasn't born yesterday.' 'Away-erthon, man, what d'ye take me fir?' 'Awayerthon, I'm not as green as I'm cabbage lookin, so I'm nat.'

awayon, 1. request to desist, to lay off: 'Awayon and take yirself aff. 'Awayon an claw moul on yirself.' 2. indication of departure: 'Am awayon ni. Goodnight.' 'Am awayon home.'

axit, door used for departure: 'I'm luckin for the axit out.' 'I cudden move for the axit was thick with people.'

14

 **bad scran,** bad luck, indicates disapproval: 'Bad scran to ye. Will ye get outa my road?'

bake, mouth, face: 'He always has his bake buried in the paper.' 'She toul me to shut my bake. I tole her she was pig iggerant.' 'When we're on our holidays I keep tellin him to hold his wee bake up till the sun.'

bakka beyond, remote, out-of-sight, distant: 'Sure their new house is at the bakka beyond.'

Ballet, abbreviation for 'William': 'Are Ballet's a bittava geg.' 'Ballet futted it the whole way without a murmur.'

Ballymena anthem, ironic Co Antrim description of 'What's in it for me?': 'Ast him to lenn ye a haun and you'll soon hear him at the Ballymena anthem.'

bap, bread roll: 'One toasted bap for his piece wud nivver satisfy our Alex. He hez t'hv thee.' 'After the wee girl got that bump on her head it was up like a bap.' 2. head: 'Don't lose yer bap over a wee thing like that. See **affis bap.**

barge, scold, abuse: 'She's only an oul barge.' 'Sure she barged the head aff me.'

barn, an exception: 'They all got samwitches barn me.' 'Everybody was there barn wee Sammy for he was sick.'

barney, 1. head, mind: 'Don't bother your barney.' 2. chat: 'We had a bit of a barney about old times.'

15

bat, blink, close one's eyes: 'A didnae bat an een all night.'

battle, bottle: 'D'ye want the sweeties outaffa battle or outaffa bax?' 'I'll have a battle by the neck.' 'I went to the chemist for a battle for my head and he ast me if I'd take it now. I said I'd wait till I got home and he gave me an awful funny look.'

baxer, pugilist: 'Geordie's a great wee baxer. Nivver gives in.' 'Are youngest says he wants to be a baxer when he grows up. He says he'll soon learn the ropes.'

beagle's gowl, denotes proximity, within hearing of the barking beagles during a hunt: 'I told him he wasn't within a beagle's gowl of the price I was lookin for the car.'

beara chews, footwear: 'I tole the man I wanted a beara chews for wearin.' 'See them beara chews? I bought them last week and they're lettin in already.' 'Them beara chews I got, the groun's started to come up through them.'

beelie, domestic cat: 'I caught my death of coul puttin the beelie out.'

beelin, suppurating, festering: 'The wee mite's heel was beelin.' 'I kept the wee lad from school for his finger was beelin.'

beezer, indicates excellence, approval: 'His drive from the first tee was a real beezer.' 'That goal was a beezer.'

bertie greetings, birthday good wishes: 'I gat bertie greetins on the radio.' 'Ye get sick listenin to them bertie greetins on the wireless.'

be-to-be, inevitable, unavoidable: 'Nathin you can do about it. Watter under the bridge. It be-to-be.'

bick, reverse, get back: 'Bick away there. Yer clear.' 'When a say "bick away" it means a want ye to bick away. Putter inta reverse.'

big, close, intimate, good friends: 'Him and her's got very big.' 'They've been big for a long time now, them two.'

binlid, stupid person: 'That fella's a binlid. I don't know what Minnie sees in him.' 'They were all binlids at the match last night.'

birl, dance expertly, nimbly: 'Armay can birl her leg.'

bisileek, bicycle: 'Alec's a great man for the bisileek.' 'I'm thinking of buyin him a pair of bisileek clips for his birthday.' 'I told the boss I was late because my bisileek started to kick up.'

bistick, biscuit: 'She gave me a cardboard tin of bisticks.' 'Ye used to be able to buy broken bisticks for next till nathin. Ni ye have to break them yerself and ye don't save a penny.'

bite, meal: 'I'm away down to my ma-in-law's for a bite.'

bittava, slight, sometimes used ironically: 'He's a bittava lad.' 'He's a bittava ijit.' 'He's a bittava geg.'

biz, is, act of being: 'If all biz well I'll be there.'

blackmouth, a Presbyterian, now little used.

blarge, crash into, behave roughly: 'She wasn't lookin where she was goin; that's why she blarged intil me.' 'I told him to take care or he'd blarge intil me.'

blether, garrulous person: 'Him, he'd blether the ears aff ye.' 'She's nathin but an oul blether. Nivver shuts up.'

blethercumskite, person who talks stupidly. See **blether.**

bley, dun coloured, pale and wan looking: 'Ye cud see she wasn't well. Her face was bley.'

bline-as-a-bat, indicates defective vision: 'The referee was as bline-as-a-bat.'

blinge, 1. drinking bout: 'He's been on the blinge for a whole week.' 2. hard blow: 'He gave him a right blinge. I wonder what came over him?'

blingle, bilingual: 'The wee girl's quaren good at the French. She's goin to be blingle.'

blink, unlucky person, apt to cast a shadow on proceedings: 'Don't ast him to come along. He's the blink.'

blirt, untrustworthy person, someone of poor character: 'The minnit I clapped eyes on him I knew he was a right blirt.' 'Onny a blirt wud act the way he behaved to my wee sister.'

boast, hollow: 'The Easter eggs I paid good money fer wuz all boast.'

boggin, untidy, unclean: 'The house was boggin so it was.' 'She's awful through-other. The place is always boggin.'

boke, vomit: 'The chile was bokin all night.' 'The way he kept chandering on and on nearly made me boke.'

bollox, muddle: 'You can bank on it. She'll make a bollox of the whole thing.' 'I spent hours explaining what it was all about but at the heels of the hunt she made a complete bollox of it.'

bookie, 1. bookmaker: 'Ye shud see the house my bookie's livin in. Onny for me he'd be livin in a hut.' 2. bunch of flowers: 'I cudden believe my eyes when he bought me a bookie for my birthday.'

booley, bandy: 'He's all booley-legged.'

borr, 1. borrow: 'I'd far rarr borr the farr's car.' 'I was onny in the house two mints when she was at the dure wantin to borr a quarter of tea.' 2. brother: 'His big borr takes the wee lad everywhere.' 3. bother: 'I told her to nivver borr her head.'

botch, carry out a task inefficiently, carelessly: 'He made a right botch of the job.' 'Ye wudden believe the botch he made of paprin the room.'

boul, 1. dish in which food is served: 'Nathin bates a good boul of parritch.' 2. cheeky, forward: 'She's a boul wee girl.' 3. lively person who is good company: 'The boul Harry was there as large as life.' 'It'll be all right once the boul Alex arrives.'

bout ye, greeting, an inquiry about your health; an indication of interest in your welfare; curiosity about your plans: 'How's bout ye?' 'Bout ye? An where d'ye think yer fir?' 'Bout ye, Jimmy. How's everything?'

boxty, dish consisting of grated potatoes, with flour and water added, then fried: 'A pan of boxty at night does a body a power of good.'

brattle, clap of thunder: 'I don't mine the lightnin. I can't stand the brattle of the thunder.'

brave, 1. more than just a few, considerable amount or distance: 'It's a brave wee bit down the road.' 2. indicative of a person of good character: 'She's a brave wee woman.' 3. descriptive of reasonable weather: 'It's a brave day.' 4. Not excessive: 'I'm feeling a brave bit better but I'm not right yet.'

bravely, 1. intoxicated but still in control, unlikely to survive a breath test: 'He was out for a fight for he was bravely.' 'I knew he was bravely when he ast me what I was hevvin.' 2. recovering from illness: 'After him being so bad he's doin bravely.'

braven offen, frequently, with regularity: 'She comes here braven offen.' 'Aye. I see him braven offen.'

braven worm, even temperature, tending to humidity: 'It's braven worm after the way it was yesterday.' 'It was braven worm this morning but its couler ni.'

breed, staff of life: 'The breed nowadays isn't what it was.' 'I always buy sliced breed. It saves ye cuttin it up.'

brew, employment exchange, unemployment benefit: 'My heart's broke trampin up and down to the brew.' 'Sure he spends more time at the brew than he does in his bed.' 'Goin aff the brew! That'll be the day.'

brock, leavings, suitable for pig feed: 'She was hingin on till his arm like a bucket of brock.'

bronical, victim of a bronchial condition: 'The oul lad's got terrible bronical trouble.' 'He's been bronical for years now.'

broughan, porridge: 'Nathin fills ye of a mornin than a bowl of hot broughan.'

brow, borrow: 'He wanted to brow our whitewash brush. He said he wanted to whitewash the yard wall blue.' See **borr.**

brunchle, a good handful, generous amount: 'I'll say this about Minnie. She'll always give ye a good brunchle.'

brung, brought, conveyed: 'He plays with the head, that boy. He brung her to the dance in his car.'

brusted, burst, punctured: 'Da, my balloon's brusted.'

19

buckijit, extreme type of idiot: 'That man's nathin but a buckijit.' 'I'm not goin to the match the day. The goalkeeper's nathin but a buckijit.' See **ijit** and **stupa ijit**.

bully, denotes approval, admiration: 'Bully Jimmy. How're ye feelin?'

bulk, flick with the fingers as in playing marbles: 'When I was a wee lad I wud bulk marleys all the time.'

bumsker, bomb scare: 'The traffic was held up because of a bumsker.' 'I'd a been here earlier onny there was an oul bumsker.'

bunnelascrap, worthless, used car: 'He tried to sell me a bunnelascrap. I ast him what did he take me for.'

bunse up, pool resources, go Dutch: 'I said I'd go with the others for a feed but only if we bunsed up.' 'We bunsed up and bought the scout-master a present.'

burr, butter: 'I always say ye can't bate country burr on yir bread.'

butterin up, flattering, cajoling: 'He's always butterin me up. Makes me sick.' 'He's a dab hand when it comes to butterin ye up.'

butt packet, pocket in a suit for small change or unfinished cigarettes: 'My butt packet's always full av butts.' 'Ye shud see my man's butt packet. It's like a midden.'

by the neck, used when ordering bottle of stout or beer, indicating that it should not be poured into a glass: 'Gawd but I have a thirst on me. A battle by the neck.'

cahee, laugh boisterously: 'They were caheein the whole night. The neighbours rapped on the wall.' 'Ye cud have heard the cahees of them a mile away.'

call, reason, excuse: 'There's no call for you to behave to me like that.' 'You've no call to spend all that money on rubbitch.'

callstanes, gall-bladder ailment: 'I nivver saw anything like her callstanes. If she brings them home she cud pebble dash the house with them.'

callus state, wake me at eight: 'Callus state for a hafta be at my work early.'

Car Door, a village in Co Down: 'Them two have lived in Car Door all their lives.' 'Quiet wee place Car Door, except when they have their motor bicycle race.'

carl singer, Christmastide vocalist: 'He's nivver in when its Christmas for he's a great wee carl singer.' 'When Christmas comes and they want a carl singer he's yer man. He just loves a cumallye.'

cast up, remember unkindly, accusingly: 'She cast up that oul jumper she gave me last year.' 'He's a divil and a half. He even cast up the trousers I didden give him for his birthday.'

catch yerself on, counsel of caution, warning against acting without considering the consequences: 'For God's sake use yer loaf. Catch yerself on, man.' 'I'll give ye the rounds of the kitchen if ye doan catch yerself on.'

21

cause girl, member of the chorus, professional dancer: 'She's onny a cause girl.' 'She's a grate kicker, a born cause girl.'

caution, 1. someone who is good company: 'She's a caution so she is. You should hear her.' 2. person to be wary of: 'Thon lad's worth watchin. He's a bit of a caution.'

champ, mashed potatoes, Ulster style: 'Shure nobody cud bate a good feed of champ.' 'That woman's champ fairly sticks to yir ribs.'

chander, bicker, quarrel, talk disagreeably: 'Chanderin's about the only thing that woman's any good at.' 'She's my sister-in-law and she's onny happy when she's chanderin.'

chaps, fried potatoes: 'Give him a plate of chaps an he's as happy as Larry.' 'My man just can't stand vinegar on his chaps. He goes for the salt, tho.'

cheesers, chestnuts, conkers: 'The wee lad loves playing cheesers.'

chegh, word used when herding a cow: 'The wee lad said he wanted to chegh the heifer intil the byre. He's a great wee help on the farm.'

cherry octopus, chiropodist: 'I wanted to go to the ospill to see the cherry octopus but I decided my fut cud hold on for anor week.' 'She's a great cherry octopus. Onny for her my feet wud hev left me.'

childer, offspring: 'Them childer wud drive ye astray so they wud.' 'The childer are a quare haunful.'

chile, infant: 'The wee chile's cryin her eyes out.' 'Just luck at her. The chile's a wee bunnel.'

chimley, chimney: 'That's the second time this week the chimley's went on fire.'

chokin, causing amusement: 'He tole me his shap was burgled and I said to him, "Yer chokin".' 'I was sure he was chokin when he said he'd won at the pools.'

clabber, wet, soft earth; mud: 'He was clabber up to the oxters.' 'There was clabber everywhere; it was shackin wire.'

clammy, uncomfortably hot, humid: 'It's an offal clammy oul day.' 'His hands were all clammy.'

clap, cow dung: 'I hate goin near that farm. I'm always walkin in cow clap.'

clart, untidy woman, through-other housewife: 'You should see that house of hers. She's nathin but a clart.'

clashbeg, tell-tale, person incapable of keeping a confidence: Ye cudden tell that one anythin. She's nathin but a clashbeg.'

clatter, 1. loud noise: 'She came a right clatter down the stairs.' 'You could hear the clatter he made a mile away.' 2. large quantity: 'She gave me a whole clatter of them.' 'I onny wanted two or three but I got a whole clatter.'

clatterbox, gossip, person incapable of keeping a secret, victim of a weakness for talking about other people's affairs: 'She's a born clatterbox.' 'She's that big a clatterbox you daren't tell her anything.'

clertma, emphatic declaration: 'Clertma goodness he tuk the light from my eyes when he drive me to the dance.'

clever, roomy, well-fitting, generously-cut garment: 'The coat she made me was that clever ye could camp out in it.' 'The suit was far too clever for him. He looked like a drowned rat.'

clinker, superbly good: 'That was a clinker of a shot you played.' See **clinkin**.

clinkin, first class: 'She's a clinkin wee dancer.' 'It was clinkin at the disco last night.' 'I had a clinkin time on my holidays.'

clipe, sizeable portion, considerable quantity: 'He has a right clipe of land.' 'I ast the grocer to give me a clipe of them ham bones.'

clockin, sitting, squatting: 'He sits clockin in front of the fire all day.' 'She sits at the winda like a clockin hen. She misses nathin.'

cloddin, throwing: 'They were cloddin petral bombs the whole night.' 'It's terrible the way they keep cloddin breeks at the police.'

clogher, cough violently and frequently: 'I'm goin to the chemist for something to stop my clogher.' 'He does nathin but sit there clogherin.' 'He has a clogher the like of which nobody ever heard before.'

clone, scent: 'I bought the missus a battle of clone to keep her quiet.'

23

clutey, left-handed, awkward: 'He can do nathin right. He's all clutey.' 'He's just like his da, clutey.'

cod, foolish individual, practical joker: 'He's onny an oul cod.' 'I tole him he was trying to make a cod outa me an I wudden stann it.'

cog, copy, imitate: 'Givvus a cog of your homework.'

coggley, unsteady, liable to collapse: 'This table's awful coggley.' 'When I wear them stillety heels it makes me feel awful coggley.'

cold fool, chicken served cold. 'Cold fool makes an awful nice bittava meal.'

collogue, converse intimately or in secret; a scheming exchange of confidences or gossip: 'The two of them is always colloguing.'

colour, small amount: 'Could I borrow a wee colour of milk.' 'I never take much milk in my tea. Just a wee colour.'

comestibles, food, provisions: 'I'll say this, she always has plenty of comestibles in the house.'

conservative, greenhouse: 'We have a wee conservative in the garden.' 'Harry gets great value outa the tomatoes he grows in the conservative.'

coorse Christian, rough diamond, person lacking in refinement: 'He's a coorse Christian if ivver there was one.'

corforus, request to be called for: 'Cud ye corforus atate?' 'He said he'd corforus and I know he'll keep his word. If he doesn't I'll show him the back of my haun.'

corned, cake or loaf baked with currants: 'I want a corned loaf.' 'Ye cudden bate a corned square.'

coul coort, indifferent, undemonstrative lover: 'He was a coul coort. I cud have kicked myself.'

coulter, sharp, cutting blade of a ploughshare: 'She has a nose like a coulter.'

24

cowboy, chancer, someone of dubious character: 'That fella's a right cowboy.' 'Thon was no football team. Nathin but a bunch of cowboys.'

cowerdy custert, person lacking in courage: 'Sure he's onny a wee cowardy custert.' 'When I raised my haun till him he tuk to his heels. A cowerdy custert.'

cowlrife, susceptible to the cold; shivery person: 'She's terrible cowlrife.' See **ashy pot.**

cowl swate, state of anxiety: 'I broke into a cowl swate when I saw the peelers.' 'We were both late for work and I was in a cowl swate when she said to me "Come on to hell Lizzie or the gates 'll be shut".'

cowp, overturn, upset: 'He cowped her intil the sheugh.'

crabbit, irascible, ill-tempered, carnaptious: 'He's that crabbit you wudden credit it.' 'She's as crabbit as the day and the marra.'

crack, lively, entertaining chat: 'Come on on in and givvus a bit of yer crack.' 'Jimmy's the quare crack.'

cratur, whiskey: 'It's hard to bate a wee drap of the cratur.' 'A wee mouthful of the cratur wud do ye no harm.'

creashy, dish for which dripping has been lavishly used: 'Thon supper was lovely an creashy.'

creepie, stool with three legs, steadier than the traditional four on an uneven cottage floor.

cribbin, kerb: 'I crigged my toe on the cribbin.' 'I was stannin on the cribbin waitin for somebody to take my arm across the road.'

croppen for all corn, someone expecting a meal, always hoping to be treated: 'Keep yer eyes skinned. She's croppen for all corn.' 'After buyin him two drinks I saw he was an oul croppen for all corn.'

cryin buckets, weeping bitterly: 'She was that upset she was cryin buckets.' 'She's awful touchy. He has onny to give her a cross look an she's cryin buckets.'

cumallye, folk song; musical house party: 'We'll have a bit of a cumallye to celebrate.' 'He sung his heart out at the cumallye last night. We were there till all hours.'

25

cut, 1. mortified, insulted, embarrassed: 'I was all cut after the things he said about me. He's very cuttin.' 'He tore intil her. She was all cut.' 'She cut me to the bone in Royal Avenue so she did.' 2. intoxicated: 'Ye cud see by the way he walked that he was half cut.'

cutty, little girl: 'She's a quiet wee cutty. Ye cudden help but tak till her.'

 **dab,** expert, possessor of considerable skill: 'She's a dab hand at the bakin.' 'He's a dab hand as a full back.'

dacent spud, likeable character, reliable person: 'I'll say this about Joe, he's one dacent spud.' 'No matter what ye hev to say about her, I can tell ye her man's a dacent spud.'

dander, 1. leisurely stroll: 'John's just gone out for a wee bit of a dander.' 2. temper: 'She always gets my dander up. She's a terrible woman.'

dawdle, short distance, simple task: 'Sure it was only a wee dawdle down the road.' 'That job was just a dawdle.'

day dawn, exactly in position: 'Them two enns of the pipe hev to be day dawn.'

dayligone, twilight, dusk: 'I love just sitting at dayligone thinkin long.'

day mare, popular daily newspaper: 'I always buy the "Day Mare". I like its palitics.' 'The only two papers we read is the "Day Mare" an the "Partial Reporter".'

dead enn, amused, astonished: 'He was a quare geg so he was. I tuk my dead enn at him.'

deadly crack, tremendous fun: 'We had a great night. It was deadly crack.' 'I wudden hev missed that wake. It was deadly crack from the word go.'

dear, expression of despair or deep feeling: 'Dear knows what has come over the wee girl.' 'Dear a dear but I feel awful. My head's turned.'

deed, deceased: 'His wife's deed this twelve month.' 'Her husband's deed an gone.' 'That fella's deed from the neck up.'

deeve, to deafen, annoy: 'The wireless was that loud it wud deeve ye.' 'It wasn't much of a party. I was just deeved the way they behaved.'

denise, niece: 'I brought denise with me.' 'Denise is a great wee dancer.'

detergent, preventive, cause of discouragement: 'A policeman on the beat is a great detergent.' 'The best detergent is a peeler roun the corner.'

dialect, abandoned, deserted: 'They're all dialect houses in that street.' 'I tole the rent collector he hadda nerve astin me to pay just to live in a dialect house.'

diclas, absurd, preposterous: 'Doan be diclas. You're talkin rubbitch.' 'Absolutely diclas. It's a latta nonsense.'

dig, violent blow: 'I'll give you a dig in the bake if you aren't careful.' 'When I gave him a dig it brought him to his senses.'

dinge, damage, dent: 'You can see the dinge where he hut my car at the corner.' 'I got a dinged tin of peas and I'm not goin to pay for them.'

dinger, indicates speed, rapidity of action: 'When I saw him he was goin a right dinger.' 'I knew he'd hit something. He was goin a dinger when he went roun the corner.'

dinnel, throbbing or tingling pain: 'I have a dinnel in my hinch.'

dinnelin, trembling, state of a child's hand on a bitingly cold day: 'It was gie coul. The wee girl's hauns were dinnelin.'

dip, fried bread: 'My man's dyin about dip.' 'Sure ye cudden bate dip bread. That's what I always say.'

dipt soda, fried soda bread: 'Dipt soda with an egg, sure ye couldn't bate it.' 'Give him two or three pieces of dipt soda and there's nathin he wudden do for you.'

28

dirt bird, contemptible, unreliable individual: 'She's a dirt bird an he's not far behind her.' 'Sure the whole fambly's nathin but a lock of dirt birds.' 'I wudden be beholden to a dirt bird like him.'

diseased, passed away: 'I knew the diseased woman terrible well. It was a lovely funeral.' 'The diseased man said if he was spared he wanted to be buried in Carmoney.'

dishabells, underclothes: 'She came to the dure in her dishabells. I didden know wherta luck.'

divid, separated, split into separate portions: 'The three of us divid the orange up, fifty fifty.' 'I always say, the world's ill divid.'

dobbin, school truancy, absenteeism: 'He was dobbin school again yesterday, the wee ruffian.'

doina line, showing affection, paying court: 'That fella's been doina line with are Minnie since Christmas.'

Doke, Doagh, village in Co Antrim: 'He comes from near Doke.'

dollop, large portion, generous helping: 'She gave me a right dollop of her stew.' 'Givvus a dollop of that champ there. I'm starvin.'

donkeys, long period of time (abbrev. of 'donkey's years'): 'I've been waiting at this bus stap for donkeys.' 'Sure my man's been breedin grewhouns fer donkeys.'

donsey, cuddly: 'She's a right donsey wee girl.'

dorient, chemical preparation to remove body odours: 'I bought him a battle av dorient for farr's day and he was all cut.' 'When the wire's hat a body needs their dorient.'

dornlaw, wife of the speaker's son: 'I ast the dornlaw up for a bite.' 'The dornlaw's very obligin.' 'The dornlaw's a right cook.'

downteel, shabby, poorly dressed: 'Ack ye cudden help feelin sorry for him. He's all downteel.'

dozer, lazy person, someone careless in behaviour and appearance: 'That fella's no dozer.' 'Keep yer eyes skinned. She's no dozer when it comes to Number One.'

drap dead, a Belfast retort: 'He said he was tryin to help and I tole him to drap dead.' 'The man ast me how he cud get to the cemetery and I tole him, drap dead.'

drapton, surprised, astonished, taken aback: 'She was fairly drapton when he walked intil the room.' 'I was drapton all right when she handed me back the poun she borrowed.'

draw, prepare a pot of tea: 'You nivver giv that tay time to draw.' 'Let the tay draw for a wee while. It's good for it.'

dree yer weird, be patient, hold your horses: 'Take yer time, man. Dree yer weird there.'

dreuth, alcoholic: 'Him? Sure he'd drink it outaffa bucket. A right dreuth.'

drib, small amount: 'I onny want a wee drib of sugar. Just as much as you'd hardly see.'

dribble, 1. small amount: 'I think I'll make a wee dribble of tay.' 'I nivver take much milk in my cup. Just a wee dribble.' 2. expert footwork during a soccer game: 'Alec was able to dribble it through the whole team. Alec's outa this world on the feel.'

drinka water, person of little account, someone considered a pain in the neck: 'He's like a long drinka water.' 'She sat there like a long drinka water.'

drippin, wet, soaked to the skin: 'It was that warm the sweat was drippin aff me.' 'He walked intil the house drippin.' 'I got caught in that shire and I'm drippin.'

drookit, wet through, soaked by rain: 'The water was pourin aff me. I was drookit.' 'Spoarin and I'm drookit.'

dropsies, game played with cigarette cards, the aim being to drop a card from a distance so that it touches or covers one already on the ground: 'When I was a wee lad we had great fun playin dropsies.' 'Member the time we played dropsies from your windey sill? Them wus the days.'

dry nod, disapproving indication of recognition: 'I just gave her a dry nod. I nivver liked the woman.'

ducle, cockerel with no fighting instincts: 'Don't bother yer head puttin money on thon ducle. You'll only lose it.'

dug, carnivorous domestic pet: 'That's a nice wee dug. Does he bark?' 'I hadda get rid of ar wee dug. He wudden give the postman peace.'

dummy tit, baby comforter: 'Give the chile her dummy tit or she'll roar the house down.' 'He lost the chile's dummy tit on me an we didden get a minnit's peace the whole night long.'

dun, tired out, exhausted: 'I've been at it since I got up an I'm dun.' 'To tell ye the truth I'm dun out. I want to get my feet up.'

duncher, cloth cap: 'It was a big funeral. There wussent a duncher to be seen.'

dunder, loud noise: 'Give her dure a dunder or she'll nivver hear ye.'

dundint, superfluous employee: 'Ever since he was made dundint he doesn't know what to do with himself.' 'It broke his heart when they told him he was dundint.'

dunt, blow: 'He hut me a quare dunt.' 'I got a dunt at the back an I onny had the car a fortnight.' 'I was stannin there mindin my own business when I gat this dunt.'

dunty, awkward, carnaptious person, unsatisfactory husband: 'He's a right oul dunty. Nivver borr yer head about him.' 'The truth is I married a dunty, Gawd help me.'

durbly, feeble, infirm: 'The aunt's got awful durbly on her feet.'

dure knacker crepe, black ribbon material used to indicate death in the house: 'She said she was goin till the shap to buy some dure knacker crape and I knew then he'd kicked the bucket.'

dynamite, jewellery: 'She lucked lovely. She was wearin dynamite earrings on her ears.'

eddick, pain, problem causing anxiety: 'Don't talk to me. I've gotta splittin eddick.' 'That fella gives me a eddick.' 'I only wish you had my eddick or you wudden be grinnin all over yer face.' 'Them rheumatic drills are an awful eddick.'

een, organ of sight: 'I didnae bat an een the whole night.' 'He's had his een on that wee girl this good while.'

Eggy, family abbrev. for 'Agnes': 'I always say Eggy has nice herr.' 'Eggy takes after me.' 'Wee Eggy has my head turned.'

ekker, school homework: 'The wee fella was sittin up till all hours doin his ekker.' 'His da's useless when it comes to givin the chile a haun with his ekker.' 'The poor wee fella can't get his ekker done with the tally blarin away there.'

enn, finish, death: 'I was foundered last night. I near got my enn.' 'One of these days he's goin to be the enn of me.' 2. extreme in amusement: 'He was quare fun. I tuk my enn at him.'

ern, journey with a specific purpose: 'Wud ye go a wee ern for me?'

esset, inquiry concerning the price of an article: 'I ast him how much esset an he give me a luck.' 'Esset dear? If it is I'm not going to borr my head.'

Extortion, type of flower: 'I'm away down till the shap to buy a packet of Extortion seed.' 'The wumman next dure always has a great show of Extortions.'

failed, in poor health, ailing: 'He looks quaren failed.' 'I tole him he needed a holiday for he was awful failed lookin.'

fairly, superlatively, excellently: 'The wee lad can fairly run.' 'She fairly tole him aff.' 'She fairly went for him.'

fairy eyes, conspicuous, prominent: 'He did it before my fairy eyes.' 'I watched her with my fairy eyes.'

falorey, lovable, mischievious person; implies harmlessness: 'He's the wee falorey man.'

fancy woman, mistress: 'Everybody knows she's been his fancy woman for years.'

farn, alien, not of British manufacture: 'They were all drivin farn cars.' 'Sure ivverybody's drivin a farn car these days.'

farr, a male parent, breadwinner: 'I'd far rarr borr the farr's car.' 'He's been a good farr to the childer.'

farry, roof-space in which to store guns and sharp tools out of reach of the children; otherwise faraway: 'Sure ye'd be in quare street without yir farry.'

fash, fish: 'I always get my fash from a man goin roun.'

Father Chart, imaginary deceased cleric: 'Our Father Chart in heaven.'

feel, venue for parade or demonstration: 'I always go to the feel on the Twelfth.'

33

feminate, not masculine: 'He had a feminate accent.'

fer, intended destination: 'Wherrer ye fer?' 'Are ye fer bed?'

fernenst, in front of: 'I can see her. She's stannin fernenst the pillar box.' 'Ye couldn't miss it. It's fernenst the Post Office.'

fernuf, acceptable, reasonable: 'What you're sayin is fernuf.' 'Fernuf, Harry. I'm game.'

ferr day, regular gathering for sale of goods or farm stock: 'It was the ferr day an everybody was there.' 'Everybody gets full on the ferr day.'

ferrdoos, shared equably: 'It was ferrdoos all roun. It's the only way.' 'Ferrdoos. I'm happy.'

ferr piece, substantial distance: 'Ye'd better get yir skates on for it's a ferr piece down the road.' 'It's a ferr piece to that new house of theirs.'

fice, front part of the head: 'He always has a fice on him that would turn a funeral.' 'Know this, that woman's fice wud scare a goat aff its tether.'

figure, attire for warm day: 'I saw her out in her figure yesterday.' 'It's far too coul to go out in yer figure.'

finaglin, dodging, scrounging: 'He's a fly man. He'd finagle his way outava strait-jacket.' 'If finaglin will get it for him he's yer boy.'

fissick, pick-me-up: 'I ast the dacter for a wee fissick for my stummick.'

fisslin, rustling noise: 'I cudden hear a word of the sermon for the fisslin in the pew behine us.'

flaffin, waving about: 'Wud ye tell yer wee girl to stap flaffin her lally?'

flannin, face cloth: 'I don't know what kine of a fambily I hev. I can nivver fine the flannin.' 'There son. Give yer wee face a rub with the flannin.' 'There's a flannin in the jawbox if ye want to wash yer face.'

flire, 1. flour: 'Them spuds is like balls of flire.' 'My favourite flire is oatmeal.' 2. flower: 'He had a wee flire in his buttonhole.'

34

flooter-futted, awkward, unskilled, esp. footballer: 'That fella's a dead loss. With a wide open goal in front of him he stans there, flooter-futted.' 'That right back's that flooter-futted he cudden even lace his boots.'

flure, floor: 'She scrubs her guts out keeping that flure spotless.'

fly man, untrustworthy person, someone to watch warily: 'Keep yer eye on that fella. He's a fly man.'

foam, telephone: 'Them foam stamps is quaren handy for futtin the bill.' 'Once she gets on the foam she'd talk yir head aff.' 'I foamed him up three times runnin.'

foe, the number above three: 'I always like a cuppa tea about foe.' 'The foe of them landed in on me outa the blue.'

fog feed, lavish meal: 'She gave him a whole fog feed.'

fonly, conditionally: 'Fonly a hadda knew about it a wudda went.' 'Fonly ye'd toul me at the time I wudden have opened my mouth.'

footer, fumbler, one who acts awkwardly: 'He's nathin but a footer.' 'He wasted the whole night footerin with a screw driver.'

forby, as well as, in addition to: 'I'll have a quarter stone of potatoes and some scallions forby.' 'Givvus a pint of milk and half a dozen eggs forby.'

foundered, chilled, suffering from exposure: 'I was foundered so I was.' 'What a night that is. I'm foundered.'

fren, companion, person with whom one is on good terms, close acquaintance: 'I've been a fren of his for years.' 'He isn't a fren. I only know him.'

fronted, insulted, mortified: 'She fronted me before the whole fambly.' 'I was nivver so fronted in my whole life.' 'I tole her I wassent there to be fronted.'

full, intoxicated, merry: 'That fella gets full at the least excuse.' 'He cudden see where he was goin for he was full to the gills.'

fummel, to fumble. See **footer.**

35

funky knuckles, awkward person, player who fails to use proper technique during a game of marbles: 'Him? Sure he's onny an oul funky knuckles. Useless.'

futless, intoxicated, incapable of walking steadily: 'He came home futless two nights runnin.'

futted, walked, travelled on foot: 'Last Twelfth I futted it every fut of the way.'

futtinit, going on a journey by foot: 'I know it's wet but I'm futtinit.' See **futted.**

**gab,** talk, chatter: 'That woman's all gab.'

galeeried, bird-brained, incapable of serious thought: 'Don't expect a word you'd understand from a galeeried character like him.'

galluses, braces: 'Don't forget yer galluses or you'll make an exhibition of yourself.'

gan, gone, going: 'She's gan hame.'

gansey, woollen jersey, sweater: 'I was sitting there a whole hour before I found my gansey had crept up on me.'

gantin, yawning: 'I tole him I was sick watching him gantin in front of the bax all night and he should get to his bed.'

gaunch, ignoramus, someone who behaves badly: 'Ye can expect nathin from a gaunch like him but bad manners.'

gebbin, talking, gossiping: 'She was stannin at the dure gebbin her head aff.' 'She nivver staps gebbin. Ye'd think the wumman was woun up.'

geek, peep, look cautiously or secretively: 'Take a wee geek and see if she's cummin.' 'I was just takin a wee geek down the street.'

geelug, earwig: 'I always give the pillow a good shake before I get intil bed. I'm dead scared of geelugs.'

geesalite, request for a light: 'Mister, cud ye geesalite?'

geg, 1. mock, poke fun at: 'She was geggin me.' 2. amusing person: 'He's a quare geg. I nearly did myself an injury laughing at him.'

37

getstuckin, start working without delay: 'You'd better getstuckin before it gets dark.' 'I told him to getstuckin or we'd never get to our beds.'

gettinmairdun, obtaining the services of a hairdresser: 'My feet's got that sore poundin roun the shops I've made up my mine. I'm gettinmairdun.'

giffover, desist: 'I wish ye'd giffover so's we can get a bitta peace.' 'I tole him to giffover but he wudden lissen.'

girn, complain, grumble incessantly: 'She's just an oul girn.'

girney gub, constantly crying child: 'Her wee lad's only a girney gub. Ye cudden satisfy the wee brat.'

gitaffye, instruction to get undressed: 'It's time to gitaffye.' 'Wud ye go and getaffye? It's after yer bedtime.'

gitonye, instruction to get dressed: 'Wud ye go and getonye? We're late.'

givverit, make it available to her: 'When yer da says givverit then givverit.' 'Givverit and stap teasin the wee girl.'

givvitadunt, hit: 'See our television? I always find if ye givvitadunt it starts.' 'That's his door. Givvitadunt there and he'll know it's us.'

givvusabit, request for a small portion: 'Givvusabit of yir orange.'

givvushare, see **givvusabit.**

glar, thick, sticky mud: 'My shoes is ruined. The road was all glar.'

gleed, 1. low light: 'You cudden see in front of you. She had hardly a gleed about the place.' 2. possessions: 'He went through his money like water. The man hasn't a gleed. Sure, his da drunk a ten acre farm. Didden ye know?'

gleek, peep: 'Take a wee gleek through the winda.'

glype, stupid, thick-headed person: 'I always said he was a born glype.' 'That fella's a glype of the worst water.'

goin strong, keeping company: 'They've been goin strong this good while.' 'That wee girl's gatta quare hoult of him. They've been goin strong for months.'

gommeril, fool, stupid person: 'He's a gommeril and that puts it in a nutshell.'

good mine, intention, resolve: 'I've a good mine to write to the paper about it.' 'I've a good mine to go and see the man face to face.'

goosegab, gooseberry: 'Sammy's mad about goosegab jam.' 'Goosegab pie's hard to bate, I always say.'

gorb, person who overeats or shows greed: 'Minnie's a greedy wee gorb.' 'Gorb? Sure she'd ate ye outa house and home.'

gorbitch, inedible food, meal not easily digested: 'She's give me a loada gorbitch for my dinner.'

gormless, silly, lacking in wit: 'The man's gormless.' See **buckijit.**

got away, died, esp. after a long illness: 'John got away last night.'

gowlin, crying, whinging: 'Her wee chile's always gowlin.' 'Give the cradle a bittava rack. Maybe that'll stop the gowlin.'

gowpen, handful, as much as can be held in the hand: 'Cud ye lenn us a gowpen of male?'

great, 1. on friendly terms: 'They fell out but himinhur's great again.' 2. considerable: 'The picture was great. I cried my eyes out.' 'Thon wee comedian was great.'

greet, cry, weep: 'What d'ye want to greet for? That won't bring the poor man's leg back.' 'Her ma was greetin all through the weddin. You'd have thought it was a wake.'

griddle, cooking utensil, used particularly for baking soda bread: 'When she has the griddle on the smell of thon soda bread wud melt a heart of stone.'

gub, mouth: 'Wud ye shut yer gub?' 'He hut me a blow on the gub.'

guess, used for cooking; type of cooker: 'I'd farr rarr have guess than the lektrick.' 'One thing about our guess cooker you can nivver guess what the bill will be like.'

guff, cheek, impertinence: 'Don't give me any of yer oul guff. I won't take it from you.'

gulder, shout, call out loudly: 'She let out a gulder at me.'

39

gully, breadknife: 'Sliced bread's all right but give me my oul gully every time.'

gulpin, brainless person, lacking in intelligence: 'The minnit I set eyes on him I knew he was a gulpin.'

gumboil, swelling on the cheek: 'She asked the chemist could he give her something for a gumboil in her hinch.'

gunk, disappointment, failure to reach expectations: 'He got a quare gunk when I didn't turn up.' 'When he heard I wasn't going to have anything to do with him he got a bit of a gunk.'

gunterpake, silly person, fool: 'What else wud ye expect from a gunterpake but stupidity?'

guttery, muddy: 'The streets is all guttery. My stackins is all japped.'

gutties, plimsolls, gym shoes: 'He's away for a run roun the corner in his gutties. The man has no sense.'

gyanbad, seriously ill: 'He's gyanbad. Even when the dog went into the room it kep its tail between its legs.'

gye, considerable: 'This parcel's gye and heavy.'

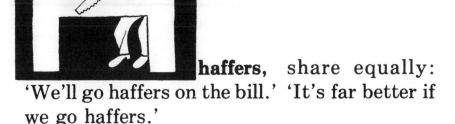 **haffers,** share equally: 'We'll go haffers on the bill.' 'It's far better if we go haffers.'

haffun, standard spirit measure: 'We'll sit down over a haffun an see how we stann.' 'Sure a wee haffun nivver done anybody a bit of harm.'

half ture, intoxicated but not quite drunk: 'Listenin to the way he was talkin ye could tell he was half ture.'

hallion, irresponsible person, good for nothing: 'They were runnin roun like a crowd of hallions.'

happed up, wrapped up cosily, tucked in: 'Is the baby happed up?' 'The wee lad's happed up fer the night. Now I can get my feet up.'

hard chaw, rough, uncouth character: 'Thon fella doesn't know the meanin of a civil answer. He's a right hard chaw.' 'I cudden truss that boy an inch. He's a hard chaw if ivver there was one.'

harp six, turn upside down, up-end: 'I went harp six on the frosty road.' 'Sammy tripped and went harp six. You should have seen him.'

harra fillum, frightening movie: 'We saw a great harra film last night. I didden sleep a wink.' 'It's hard to bate a good harra film. If only Harry wudden go to sleep.'

harrished, tormented, harassed: 'I've been harrished the whole morning.'

hartacorn, describes generosity, warmth, forgiveness: 'There's nathin Maggie wudden do for ye. She has a real hartacorn.' 'Jimmy has a hartacorn. Sure he'd give ye the sleeves outa his waistcoat so he wud.'

hate, 1. anything: 'I don't know a hate about it.' 2. warmth: 'I cudden get any hate intil my bones. It was freezin.'

haun, hand: 'He took a right haun outa me.' 'I'll give you a bitava haun if you like.' 'Lennus a haun and don't just stann there, yer two arms the one length.'

haunless, awkward, ham-fisted: 'The man's just haunless with his feet.' 'Oul Jimmy's a haunless glype.'

hayeawlwiye, inquiry to establish if one has everything prepared for a departure: 'Are you sure ni? Hayeawlwiye? You've left nathin?'

headbin, dolt, dunderhead: 'He's nathin but a headbin.' 'I know you'll call me a headbin but I know Linfield will bate them intil the groun.'

head bomadeer, head waiter, foreman, overseer: 'Get me the head bomadeer. This stake isn't fit for a dog.' 'Hurry up, Jimmy, or the head bomadeer'll go fer ye.'

head-the-ball, unpredictable person, someone liable to make stupid decisions: 'Don't listen to a word he says. He nathin but a head-the-ball.'

heart scalded, bothered, troubled, harassed: 'That wee girl has my heart scalded.'

heavy metal, exclamation indicating astonishment, warning of impending disaster: 'Heavy metal! You don't say.' 'Heavy metal! Wud ye watch where yer goin.'

heesawun, a character, one who draws attention to himself: 'Heesawun. He always was a bit of a boyo.'

heff iate, eight-thirty (esp. in Ballymena): 'I'll be along about heff iate.'

he hadda view, intoxicated: 'Ye cud tell he hadda view. He was talkin funny.' 'Anybody cud see he hadda view. I wud hev said he was stovin.' 'He hadda view all right for as far as I cud see the man was futless.'

42

hellferlire, going at full speed, in a hurry: 'I saw him going hellferlire down the road.' 'The fella flew past me, hellferlire.'

hennae, denies possession: 'A hennae onny.' 'He says I hennae an ounce of sense. Imagine sayin a thing like that!'

hepney, coin which vanished with metrication: 'When I was a wee lad I used to buy a hepney worth of liquorice allsorts. They were lovely.'

herr, growth on the head: 'She has awful nice herr.' 'I'm away to get my herr done.'

heswainthead, someone who has lost his senses: 'Don't heed him. Sure heswainthead.'

hice, house, home: 'We have an awful nice we hice ni.' 'She lives in a funny hice. The front door's at the back.'

hiltnirhare, evidence of existence or presence: 'I saw nire hiltnirhare of them.' 'I looked high and low but there wasn't hiltnirhare of them.'

himinhur, married couple, sweethearts: 'Himinhur's been married over a year now.' 'Himinhur ast us down for a drink.' 'Himinhur make a right pair.'

himself, 1. husband, head of the house: 'Is it himself you want? He's weedin in the garden.' 'I'll have to have a word with himself about it.' 2. employer, boss: 'I want to see himself to see if he'll let me have the day aff.' 3. outstanding personality: 'It's himself coming on to the platform now. Isn't it great?'

hinch, upper part of the human leg, thigh: 'I tole the dacter I had a pain on my hinch.'

hirple, limp, walk with difficulty: 'He can hardly hirple down the road.' 'I watched him hirple past the dure this morning. I gotta laff.'

hiyew, exclamation demanding attention: 'Hiyew, who do you think you are?' 'Hiyew. Am I right for Chadally Street?'

hoke, scoop out: 'Wait a minute till I hoke out the fire.'

hough, breathe heavily, expel warm breath: 'Wud ye hough on the winda? It's all steamed up.'

43

howl awn, advice to take your time, not to be too hasty: 'Howl awn there till we see what's what.' 'Wud ye howl awn for a minnit? There's no desprit hurry.'

huffs, thighs: 'Didye see her skirt? It was away up till her huffs.'

hug-me-tight, shawl that can be fastened, woollen vest: 'It was that coul she wore her hug-me-tight in bed.'

huir inna Honda, careless driver of a foreign car: 'I was giv a dunt by a huir inna Honda and I onny had the car a week.' 'A huir in a Honda backed intil me and nivver had the dacency to stap. Make ye spit.'

hunkers, heels: 'He was sittin there onnis hunkers.' 'She was down on her hunkers in front of the fire.'

hurstle, hoarseness: 'I have a wee bittava hurstle.'

hurwuns, wife's relations: 'When hurwuns come ye can't hear yir ears. Everyone of them has talk for two rowsa teeth.' 'Hurwuns wud ate ye outa house an home.'

hut, hit, deliver a sharp blow: 'He hut me in the face so he did.' 'I didn't open my mouth but he hut me in the eye.'

 **iggerant,** uneducated: 'He's as iggerant as sin.'

ijit, idiot, stupid person: 'He's an oul ijit and I tole him so till his face.' See **buckijit.**

incentative, an encouragement to action or effort: 'There's no incentative to do a day's work nowadays.'

intended, fiancée: 'I suppose you and your intended will be at the dance?'

ires, long period of time: 'He clocks in front of the fire for ires on enn.' 'I was waiting for him for ires. I fairly lit intil him.'

irn, smoothing iron: 'I always irn of a Friday.' 'I'll have to go in and irn.'

ironaf, fixed period of time: 'I always get an ironaf for my lunch.' 'I've been stannin her waitin fer ye for a good ironaf.'

italiation, revenge for an insult or injury: 'I hut him in italiation.' 'They wudden let him intil the house and he set it on fire in italiation.'

jacked duncher, cloth cap with checked pattern: 'He was all dressed up in his jacked duncher.' 'He was at the match on Sardy. I saw his jacked duncher.'

jamember, request to recollect: 'Jamember the day we went to Bangor and you nearly cowped the wee boat?' 'Jamember when ye cud get to Bangor and back for a bob?'

japped, muddied: 'The road was that guttery after the rain that I got my tights all japped.' 'Them japs is terrible hard on yer nylons.'

jar, drink (esp. alcoholic): 'Ye'll have a wee jar afore ye go.' 'We've time for a jar, haven't we?'

jawbox, kitchen sink: 'Put the dishes in the jawbox, wud ye?' 'Me? Sure I spend half my life stannin at the jawbox.'

job, illegal activity: 'He was out on a job last night. Blew up three shaps anna Cartina.' 'I saw the armalite under his coat so he must be goin out onna job.'

joinin, rebuke, chastise: 'The next time I set eyes on that wee targe I'll give her a good joinin.' 'He give me a terrible joinin when all I was doin was makin faces at him.'

jorum, measure of liquor, depending on the generosity of the pourer: 'Houl on, man, and we'll have a wee jorum.'

jubilant, juvenile: 'She's a jubilant delinquent.'

juke, dodge, elude: 'He juked roun the corner.' 'When its his turn to stan a roun he's a dab haun at jukin ye.'

juke-the-beetle, poor cook: 'Her champ's always full of lumps. The woman's just a juke-the-beetle.'

juke-the-bottle, teetotaller: 'Don't be astin him along. He's onny an oul juke-the-bottle.'

jundered, jostled: 'He jundered his way through. I nearly went harp six on the flure.'

 **kack-handed,** left-handed,
awkward: 'He's no carpenter and nivver was.
He's that kack-handed you wouldn't credit it.'

kaileyin, party-going, having a good time, going from one ceilidhe to another, gossiping: 'All he does is go kaileyin every night.' 'She's been kaileyin every night for the last month.' 'Her tongue nivver stops. All she thinks of its kaileyin.'

ken, 1. know, be acquainted with: 'A ken him well.' 'He came intil our ken a good wee while back.' 2. utensil used for making tea, esp. by shipyardmen: 'I'll boil yir ken for ye.'

kent, had knowledge of: 'A kent him well.' 'A kent John for the last forty year.' See **ken.**

kep, 1. flat-topped forage cap with a straight peak: 'His kep blew aff in the gale.' 2. retain: 'A kep it because he gave it to me.'

kidleys, kidneys: 'Alec's having bother with his kidleys. It's the drink.'

kileery, light-headed: 'She's a wee kileery. Hasn't an ounce.'

kitchen, comfort: 'Butter to butter's no kitchen' (said of two girls dancing together).

kitterdy, giddy, foolish person: 'She's nathin but a wee kitterdy.'

knawky, cunning, crafty: 'Keep your eyes skinned. She's as knawky as the divil himself.'

knee-cap, terrorist punishment, on suspected informers, by shooting victims in both knees: 'Wee Sammy's been knee-capped twice. He's had a terrible time of it, the sowl.'

know-all, superior person, someone who knows everything: 'Her? She's an oul know-all.' 'If anybody can put ye right it's Cissy. She's the know-all of the family.'

knowin, small amount, what you would know to be there: 'Cud ye lennus a wee knowin of sugar?'

kyart, 1. horse drawn vehicle: 'If you don't watch out you'll cowp the oul kyart intil the sheugh.' 'Keep yer eye out fir thon corner or you'll cowp the kyart, load an all.' 2. difficulty, dilemma: 'The man has the mine of a wee lad. I knew he'd finish up in the kyart.'

 **lacin,** beating: 'He gave the wee lad a quare lacin.' 'My da give me a lacin for scuffin my new shoes.'

lack, like, similar to: 'Lack ye know.' 'The wee lad's awful lack his farr's side of the house.'

laid up, unwell, confined to bed with illness: 'He's been laid up this fortnight.' 'Seeing she's laid up I'll hafta get her a buncha grapes.'

lake, leak: 'The teacher asked her what a lake was and she said it was a hole in a kettle.'

lally, lollipop: 'The child was flaffin her lally all over her good new dress.'

larn, teach, acquire knowledge, study: 'That'll larn ye nivver for till do that again.' 'She's goin till night classes till larn French.' 'The wee lad always brings out his books when I tell him he hasta larn his lessons.'

larry, delivery vehicle, truck: 'I got them for next to nathin. They fellaffa larry.' 'The wee fella fellafa larry an hurt himself.'

lat, large amount: 'He gave me a quare lat.' 'It takes a quare lat of ijits to fill Windsor Park.'

lather, ladder: 'The winda cleaner fell aff is lather.'

lennusahaun: request for assistance: 'For God's sake wud ye lennusahaun with this table?'

lennusapoun, request for a loan: 'Ye cudden lennusapoun cud ye? Till Friday?' 'He says to me "Cud ye lennusapoun?" I tole him to get stuffed.'

lenthamatung, reprimand, reproach: 'I give him the lenthamatung. He ast for it.'

leppin, 1. throbbing painfully: 'My corns is leppin.' 'I can't sleep with my sore knee. It starts leppin the minnit I get into bed.' 2. jumping on horseback: 'The mare was fairly leppin.' 'We're going to see the leppin on Saturday.'

lettin in, leaking: 'My shoes are lettin in.'

lettin on, pretending: 'I knew rightly she didn't mean what she said. I knew she was onny lettin on.'

letton, reveal, disclose: 'Nivver letton ye saw me.' 'He knew but he nivver letton.'

liarintit, invitation to begin a meal, eat heartily: 'Liarintit. It'll warm the cockles of yir heart.' 'See my man? Make him a fog feed and ye don't have to tell him to liarintit.'

lift, understand, grasp the meaning of: 'She's onny two but that wee girl can lift me.' 'I listened to him for ires but I cudden lift a single word.'

lifted, 1. arrested, taken into custody by police: 'He was lifted twice in the one week.' 'The peelers must be sick of the sight of him. They lifted him again last night.' 2. assisted, helped up after a fall: 'Listen and I'll explain what happened. Dickey was lifted, but he wasn't taken to any police barracks. He was lifted because he fell.'

lig, fool, light-hearted person: 'She's always actin the lig.'

like hisself, little changed, of normal appearance: 'I was up lookin at the corpse. He's awful like hisself.' 'She was bad for a long time but when I saw her in the coffin she was awful like herself.'

likkinapramise, clean a room hastily, incompletely: 'I give the house a likkinapramise.' 'Just give the flure a likkinapramise until we get back.'

lilties, people who act foolishly, irresponsibly: 'I saw the two of them goin down the road like a perr of lilties that didden know day from night.'

lion upstairs, in bed, not yet awake: 'Wud ye luck at the time and him still lion upstairs.' 'Lion upstairs? That's a question to ask at levin in the morning.'

lippit, taste: 'I made him a bowl of onion soup but the oul divil wudden lippit.' 'I offered her panada but she just wudden lippit. Sure I keep telling her to eat it up but it just goes in one ear and out the other.'

loaf, intelligence, awareness: 'Use yer loaf, man.' 'You get nowhere in this world if you don't use yer loaf.'

lock, considerable amount, not a small quantity: 'She gave me a good lock of them beans.' 'I ast him to give me a lock of his spuds.'

long, to desire, to yearn for happier times: 'Are you thinkin long?' 'She just sits there thinkin long. What good does that do anybody?'

lose, undo, unfasten: 'I told him not to forget to lose his laces before he wenta bed.'

low set, small of stature: 'She's a wee low set woman. When she sits down ye wudden know she was there.'

luck, stare at, behold: 'She gave me a luck that wud have turned milk.' 'Wud ye just luck at the way that woman's dressed.'

lump, growing child: 'She's a great wee lump.' 'He's a big lump of a lad now.'

maddles, term used in dressmaking and millinery trades: 'We cud do with some younger maddles.' 'Her and her sister are maddles ni but they haven't been maddlin long.' 'That hat is one of our latest wee maddles.'

make trex, bid farewell, depart after a visit: 'Slate. I'll hafta make trex.'

male, meal; breakfast, lunch, tea or dinner: 'She's a great one for four males a day.' 'He expects to see a male on the table the mint he walks in through the door.'

mands biz friz, indicates extreme cold: 'Luck at them. Mands biz friz so they are.' 'If onny I'd brought my gloves for mands biz friz.'

mane, miserly, lacking in generosity: 'Ye wudden credit how mane that fella is.' 'Mister you're on the mane road to Ballymena and the nearer you get to it the maner it gets.'

mangey, 1. skin disease in animals: 'The cat's mangey.' 2. mean, miserly: 'Don't expect anything from him. He's terrible mangey.' See **mingey.**

mantanny, aunt named Annie: 'Mantanny wud nivver ast ye if ye had a mouth on ye.' 'Mantanny won prizes at the dancin when she was a wee girl. She's very light on her feet.'

marley, marble, used in the game of marbles: 'He lost his marley down a gratin.' 'He cried his wee eyes out when he cudden fine his marley.'

meelcartins, chilblains: 'My heart's scalded with the meelcartins.'

meetin, church service: 'I ast her if she was for meetin and she gave me a look.' 'That was a great preacher at the meetin this morning. Ye cud have felt the spits of him five pews away.'

meggs, eggs of the domestic hen: 'I always like meggs hard.' 'I ast her to fry meggs for my breakfast.'

melt, indefinite part of the human body: 'I'll knock yer melt in so I will.' 'He got intil a fight and got his melt knocked in. He was good value for it.'

mended, improved in health, recovered from illness: 'Our bootmaker's awful well mended for he was at death's dure.'

minchin, trespassing: 'He keeps minchin intil our feel.'

mine, 1. remember: 'I forgot to mine my parcel.' 'D'ye mine the day we all went up the Cavehill fir a picnic an it poured?' 2. take care of, look after: 'I ast her to mine the shap.' 3. opinion, viewpoint: 'Sure he doesn't know his own mine.' 4. give heed to: 'Nivver mine him. He's nat worth botherin about.' 5. apply oneself to: 'Mine yer own business.' 6. take objection to: 'Ye wudden mine callin roun wud ye?' 7. observe, take note of: 'Mine the step.' 'Mine where ye're goin.' 8. belonging to me: 'What's his is mine and what's mine's me own.'

minexore, indicates neck pain (as distinct from 'pain in the neck'): 'I can't turn roun for minexore.'

mingey, mean, uncharitable, ungenerous: 'She's awful mingey. She wudden even give you the time of day.' 'She's that mingey they call it Christmas mourn in her house.'

mint, short period of time: 'The train goes in a couple of mints.' 'Houl yir horses. I'll onny be a mint.' 'The mint I set eyes on you I remembered.'

mismorrowed, ill-matched: 'If ivver two people were mismorrowed, it's them two.'

54

mizzle, mild rain: 'It's started to mizzle.' 'This wire wud senn ye roun the bend. It'll start to mizzle any minnit.' 'I'd left my umbrella in to be restrung and there I was, caught in the mizzle.'

monmone, unaccompanied: 'I didden come to the dance with anybody. I'm monmone.'

monney down, just out of bed: 'I'm not at myself yet. Sure monney down.' See **monney up.**

monney up, just out of bed: 'Monney up this mint.' 'Wait till I get my brain shired. Monney up.' See **monney down.**

morr, female parent: 'I'll hafta ast m'morr if she'll let me go to the party.' 'M'morr isn't up outa her bed yet.'

morrowin, borrowing a horse on the understanding that it will be returned the following day; harvest-time custom: 'I've been morrowin with Wullie John now for many a long day.' 'Onny for the morrowin I wudden know where I was.'

morr tung, native speech: 'When ye hear the morr tung in yer ears ye know yer among frens.' 'The best thing about goin home on a visit is to be able till lissen till people usin their morr tung.'

mouthful, small amount, cupful, tea not taken formally at the table: 'Wud ye like a mouthful in yer haun?' 'I'm not stayin. I'll just have a mouthful in my haun.'

mower, more, additional quantity, extra helping: 'There's mower tea in the pot if you want any.' 'You remember that song, "The Mower We Are Together"?'

muncle, brother of the speaker's father or mother: 'Muncle's a quare boyo.' 'Muncle give me a poun for my birthday.'

mutton dummies, plimsolls, gym shoes: 'Imagine! Tryin to play fut-ball in his mutton dummies!'

 **nackitaff,** stop, desist, cease: 'I tole her to nackitaff but she wudden heed me.'

nammel jug, vessel made of enamel: 'The great thing about a nammel jug is that it doesn't break if you drap it.' 'Nammel jugs always make me think of ospill.'

nattalat, small, insignificant quantity: 'What am I growin in the garden. Ack, nattalat.' 'There's nattalat in the paper the night.'

nearall, mainly, mostly: 'That tea was nearall water.' 'We'll call the meetin to order. We're nearall here ni.'

neb, nose: 'She isn't a bad sort onny she can't help puttin her neb in.' 'Every time he sneezes ye can hear his neb crakin like a whip.' 'He cud hoke a path with his neb from here till Ballyclare an nivver get a mote in his eye.'

nebby, inquisitive (usually applied to a busybody): 'She's terrible nebby.'

neg, 1. food used for making omelettes: 'It's hard to bate a neg in the pan.' 'She ast me what way I'd like a neg and I said with anor one.' 2. scold, rebuke constantly: 'She's onny an oul neg.'

neggin, 1. scolding, persistently finding fault: 'The wife nivver staps neggin me.' 2. throbbing, insistent pain or problem: 'This oul tooth kept neggin all night.' 'It's been neggin me ivver since whether I done the right thing.'

neighbour, indicates agreement with a proposed action, that it is no bother: 'It's all right. Sure it's neighbour.'

56

neuck, take without permission, steal: 'I saw the wee lad neuck one of the apples.'

ni, at the present, the present time: 'I'm goin ni.' 'Ni is the hour, as the song says.'

nire, 1. not either: 'She's isn't goin an nire am I.' 2. sixty minutes: 'I'll see ye in about a nire.' 'I've been stannin here waitin a nire so I have.' 'I was poundin roun the shaps for a nire and my feet just give up.'

nire hiltner hairaff, no sign of, no sight of: 'I lucked high an low but there was nire hilter hare of him.' 'I let the wee lad out two seconds ago an ni there's nire hiltner hairaff him.' 'Where that wee dug gets to I don't know but when I lucked there was nire hiltner hairaff him.'

nivverbor, suggests you should change your mind, take a different course of action, or do nothing: 'Nivverbor yir head.' 'If you're a wise man you'll nivverbor.' 'I tole him to nivverbor but he nivverbord listenin.'

noan, not any: 'I have noan left. They're all done.' 'Monmone in the house. There's noan of them in.'

nocker up, person who acts as professional alarm clock: 'We used to have a great wee nocker up but it was a long while ago. He'd dunder at the door until you riz.'

noddity, eccentric, someone whose behaviour is abnormal: 'I'd say he was a noddity all right. Sure the way he gets on wud show ye he hadda wee bittava want.' 'Imagine, puttin 50p. on a horse called "Fourth". Only a noddity wud do a stupid thing like that.'

no empey skite, well-fed: 'By the look of him that fella's no empey skite.' 'After what he shovelled intil him I wud say he's no empey skite.' 'After a coupla fried eggs an three farls of soda yir no empey skite.'

no goat's toe, judicious, of good sense: 'I know him well. He's no goat's toe I can tell you.'

no gra, without enthusiasm, lacking interest or appetite: 'He had no gra for his dinner.'

nopen woon, unbandaged injury to the flesh caused by blow or stab: 'There was me with a nopen woon and nobody bothered their head.' 'That man of hers has a fice like a nopen woon.'

57

Norn Iron, Northern Ireland: 'When the man called me a footer I knew I was in Norn Iron.'

nyarley fry, well-cooked fry of eggs, sausages, bacon, and soda bread: 'Ye cudden bate a nyarley fry.' 'Once he gets stuck intil a nyarley fry he's neighbour.'

nyrps, depressing thoughts, low spirits: 'That woman always gives me the nyrps.'

oan, possess: 'I don't oan this bisileek. I was lent it.'

odious, unusual, distinctive, marked: 'That's an odious fine day so it is.' 'She's an odious fine woman.'

orchin, small boy, mischievous youngster: 'He's a terrible wee orchin.' 'The wee orchin neucked an orange.'

ornje, gold-coloured citrus fruit: 'Ye cudden bate one of them chaffa ornjes.' 2. colour between red and yellow: 'I ast for a pair of ornje men's socks an the girl give me a look.'

orrday, recently, a few days ago: 'I saw her the orrday.' 'I heard about it the orrday there.'

orrdure, alternative entrance or exit: 'There was a bumskerr and we all hadda use the orrdure.' 'There was a notice that said "Use orrdure".'

ospill, place of healing: 'She's lyin in the Satty Ospill.' 'She was tuck to ospill in an amblence.' 'When you ast in the ospill they onny luck at ye. All I wanted was to fine the cherry octopus to see about my feet.'

oul, 1. ancient, venerable: 'He's a right oul age.' 'She's an oul ijit.' 'Ye cudden help but like the oul cratur.' 2. held in high regard: 'I bought this bit of an oul coat only last week. I wudden be without it.'

oulig, old fool, aged idiot: 'He's an oulig. Ye'd think he'd know better at his time of life.'

oulip, abuse, insult: 'Don't be givvin me any of yer oulip.'

oxtercog, assist by holding under the arms: 'We hadda oxtercog the oul blether the whole way home.'

59

oxters, armpits: 'That wee woman's in debt up till her oxters.' 'Honest to Gawd, Harry, I'm up the creek up till my oxters.'

pahle, limp, move with difficulty, travel slowly and laboriously on foot: 'He's a rare sight tryin to pahle up the stairs.' 'Take it from me, Willie's nathin but a pahle. There's more life in Willie's walking stick than there is in Willie.' 'I'll pahle down till your house the night for a wee bit of yer crack.'

palaver, debate, to talk about at length, to discuss in tedious detail: 'All I got was a whole palaver about it.' 'Him and her spent the whole night on a long palaver.'

pan, 1. cooking utensil used for frying: 'The wife gives me the pan for breakfast seven times a week.' 'My sister had her stummick out last week and now she can ate anything. Last night she even ate the pan.' 2. human face: 'If you don't mine yer language I'll knock yer pan in.' 'She has a pan like a ploughed field.'

panada, bread pudding: 'She's that bad all she can ate is panada.' 'Since I got my new teeth I've been livin on panada. It's cummin outa my ears.'

pant, absurd activity: 'Did you see the pant at the corner last night?' 'There was a right pant when he walked into the house futless.'

parletic, intoxicated, thoroughly inebriated: 'He was measurin the walls last night again. Parletic up to the oxters.'

parmacy, chemist's shop: 'I'm away down to the parmacy to get some jube jubes for meers for we're flyin to London.' 'While I'm out I'll drap in at the parmacy for some moth balls for my drawers.'

parritch, popular breakfast food made by boiling oatmeal or other cereal into a thick paste: 'My man's dyin about a plate of parritch for his breakfast.' 'That wee lad has my heart broke. He won't lip his parritch.'

part, tropical bird with brilliant plumage: 'They had a part in a cage that cud say "I wanta drink".' 'My man's away out till buy seed for the part. That oul bird costs a fortune.'

passremarkin, describes a person apt to make uncomplimentary comments about others: 'I don't like her at all. She's awful pass-remarkin.'

pass yerself, behave sociably, act amiably when in company: 'I'll just have a wee drink to pass myself.'

pavilion passenger, rider on a motor-cycle pillion: 'She was his pavilion passenger when he ran intil the lamp-post.' 'It's grate fun ridin on the pavilion but it fairly ruins yer herr.'

pech, grunt, pant: 'She was pechin up the stairs.' 'The pechs of her! Ye cud hev heard them a mile away.'

pechlin, see **pahle.**

perr, a couple, husband and wife: 'There's her and her ma an they're a perr.' 'The perr of them went down the street like a couple of lilties.'

persperatin, sweating: 'I was fairly persperatin. The swate was pourin aff me.'

phrase, a stage, change, period of time: 'She's goin through one of her phrases.'

picker, person with poor appetite, one who prefers small helpings: 'I'd far rarr cook fer a gorb than a picker any day.'

piece, a worker's packed lunch: 'I got him a wee plastic beg for him to carry his piece to work.' 'He's as fussy as the day and the morra about what's in his piece.'

piggin, unclean, untidy: 'Her house is always piggin. That wumman doesn't know what a brush is for.'

piggy, street game played with small, pointed piece of wood which is propelled through the air by a stick: 'I tole the wee lads if that oul piggy went through one of my windas they'd pay for it.'

pig's back, on top of the world; indicates confidence, absolute assurance: 'After ten minnits' play the team was on the pig's back, two goals up.'

pijun-futted, sly, cunning: 'Watch that one. She's pijun futted.'

pijuns, birds of the dove family: 'He's been breedin pijuns all his life.' 'Life isn't worth livin since the man next dure started breedin pijuns. Sure they breed like rabbits.'

pitcher, film, movie: '*Gone With The Wine*'s a pitcher and a half. I cried my eyes out.' 'The big pitcher was terrible; it was a waste av good money quein up till see it.'

plane, to be involved in recreational activity, taking part in a game: 'The wee lad's out plane in the street.' 'The childer were plane tig all day.'

plaster, hypocrite: 'He's nathin but an oul plaster.' See **poultice.**

plite, courteous, well-behaved: 'He's awful plite. Pulls up his trousers when he sits down.' 'He's an obligin, plite wee man.' 'I've nivver met a plite rent collector in my whole life.'

plowterin, moving aimlessly about, acting without any particular purpose, wasting time: 'Ack, I'm onny plowtering aroun.' 'He's plowterin away there in the garden.'

Plues, Linfield Football Club: 'The wee Plues can fairly play.' 'The Plues is plane away the day.'

plugher, 1. indication of lung infection, to clear the throat noisily: 'He has an awful bad plugher.' 'Ye should hear the plughers of her. Bad chests run in the family.' 2. smoky, dusty atmosphere: 'There was a terrible plugher in the room for he was at his oul pipe.'

63

plump, sudden shower of rain: 'That was a right plump. I was wringin when I got home.'

plute, pester, annoy, aggravate: 'The chile's been plutin me all day.' 'That wee lad plutes the life outa me.'

potata clock, around eight a.m. or p.m.: 'Seeya potata clock.'

poultice, hypocrite: 'She's nathin but an oul poultice, that's what I think.'

powerful, likeable, unusual: Her husband's a powerful wee man. Ye cudden help but take to him.' 'The new minister's a powerful preacher but it's nice when he gets to thirdly.' ('Thirdly' relates to the preaching convention of having first, second and third points of progression in the discourse.)

pravins, province: 'I've been livin in the pravins all my life.' 'It wud sicken ye sometimes. The wire's that bad over the whole pravins.'

preys, potatoes: 'Them preys was lovely.' 'She give me a great plate of preys.'

prig, to make a bargain: 'If ye go to Ballymena and ye don't prig they'll think ye're mad.' 'Unless ye prig ye'll pay through the nose.'

puke, 1. to vomit, to spew: 'She was pukin all over the place. The meal didden agree with her.' 2. supercilious person, one who displays superior airs: 'She's a right puke.' 'She looked through me, the puke.'

pumlican, owner of licensed premises: 'He's a pumlican. Sure he owns two pubs.'

pumpture, motoring misfortune, tyre trouble: 'We were onny down the road ten minutes when he gatta pumpture.' 'He was in a right state when he gat his third pumpture in two days.'

purr down, refers to the movement of furniture, term used by removal men: 'Purr down ni, Jimmy.' 'Ye didden purr down when I told ye to purr down. I nearly busted a gut. What kine of a man are ye?'

puttin onner, getting dressed: 'She was onny puttin onner when I called roun.' 'The wife's upstairs puttin onner.'

quare, memorable, unusual, outstanding: 'You're a quare geg.' 'The pitcher was a quare bittava laugh.' 'It was a quare wet day. I was foundered.'

quare man m' da, indicates disbelief, an awareness that an attempt is being made to fool the hearer: 'Sole yer house? Quare man m' da!' 'Won the pools, did ye? Quare man m' da.'

Quewy, affectionate version of 'Hugh'. See **Shewy.**

quilt, objectionable, mean or disobliging person: 'She's a quilt of the deepest dye.' 'If ye want my opinion Rachel's a born quilt.' 'A quilt of the first water, that fella. He has an eye like a cold fried egg.' 'The woman's a right oul quilt. She's as cuttin as a pan loaf.'

quire, band of singers: 'She's fairly come on. She's singin in the quire ni.' 'Mary's goin with a quare nice fella. He says he's in the quire.'

ramstam, act recklessly, thoughtlessly: 'He went at it ramstam.' 'I warned the man. I tole him not to go at it ramstam.'

rapin, harvesting: 'He said he was wore out for he was rapin in the feel all day.' 'She ast him was he busy and when he said he'd been rapin for hours she took till her heels, the silly ijit.'

rare, raise, educate: 'I hadda rare three childer an I wudden do it again.'

rare crack, entertaining, lively conversation: 'It's always rare crack if he's there.' 'It was rare crack at Minnie's last night.'

rare turn, amusing person: 'She's a rare turn. I tuk my dead enn at her.' 'That fella's a rare turn. He had everybody in stitches.'

rarr, prefer: 'I'd far rarr go to the pitchers.' 'I'd rarr ye didden tell her.'

ratten, unfortunate, unpleasant: 'Yir man had a heart attack? Ack that was ratten for ye.' 'She tole me Alec had cut his throat an I said that was ratten for her.'

raut, worked: 'He raut in the shipyard all his life.' 'He nivver raut anywhere else but Mackie's.'

redd, tidy up after a party, clear the table after a meal: 'I havta go an redd up.'

rench, rinse: 'He wudden even help me to rench the dishes.' 'I can't talk to ye ni. I havta rench the clothes out.'

rentin, vomiting: 'She was rentin the night out.' See **puke.**

riftin, belching: 'We got that much to ate the ould fella was riftin like mad.'

right, used to add emphasis to a statement: 'That's a right bittava night.'

right haun, mess or muddle: 'The dog made a right haun of the garden. One of these days I'm goin to show it my boot.' 'John made a right haun of the back room. He wasted more paint than he put on.'

right ijit, stupid, senseless person: 'Charlie's a right ijit.' 'I tole him he acted like a right ijit when they ast him to stann up an sing.'

rightly, 1. merry, intoxicated: 'When I saw him he was rightly.' 'Him? Two drinks and he's rightly.' 'That fella wud get rightly on a tummler of tomato juice.' 2. prospering: 'Now he's workin he's doin rightly.'

right 'n' bad, in poor health, in a serious condition (not a reference to poor handwriting): 'I tuk him a buncha grapes for he was right 'n' bad.' 'I tole the chemist I was right 'n' bad and he said did I want a new ballpoint. Imagine!'

right one, unpredictable person: 'Keep yer eyes skinned. That boy's a right one.' 'I knew she was a right one the minnit she opened her mouth.'

right shar, fairly heavy fall of rain: 'That was a right shar. It's a good job I brought my raincoat.'

right yar, indicates agreement, approbation: ' "Ye can go on ahead." "Right yar." ' ' "See ye Sardy?" "Right yar." '

right yebe, sign of approval: 'Right yebe, Charlie. That's just dandy.' 'Ye're all right ni? Right yebe.'

rining, raining: 'It's been rining since I got up.' 'That's what's the matter with this place. It's always rining. It nivver staps.'

riotery, noisy pigs and geese in a farmyard: 'The riotery was shackin.' 'You shudda heard the riotery. It was worse than a disco.'

ritefy, confirm: 'I said I wudden pay it until he sut down to ritefy the figures.' 'Ye can't say it'll do until you get him to ritefy it.'

riz, out of bed: 'She wassent even riz when I called at the house after ten.'

rosiner, drink, a good measure of whiskey: 'You'll have a rosiner before ye go?' 'That was a right rosiner. Here's t'ye.'

rowboat, robot used by bomb disposal experts for testing purposes: 'They sent a rowboat out to see if it was a bomb an it was nathin but a hoax.'

rumplety thump, untidily, in disorder: 'She just left everythin rumplety thump.'

runt, a cabbage stalk; the weakling in a litter of pigs; undersized **person:** 'I can take a salad but not when there's a coupla runts in it.' 'He's only a wee runt of a man.'

sack, unwell, indisposed: 'I was aff sack for a whole week.' 'She's been on the sack for more nor a month.'

saft day, mild weather: 'It's that kine of day, saft.'

sallrite, indicates that all is well: 'There's nathin to worry about. I saw the house. Sallrite.' 'I hadda a luck at the new car. Sallrite, sotis.'

sally wattle, branch from a thorn hedge with the thorns removed: 'We were walkin down the loanin swishin our sally wattles.'

Sardy, Saturday: 'Are ye goin till the match on Sardy? It'll onny be a waste of good money but sure ye nivver know.'

sarky, speak ironically: 'I can't stann him, he's that sarky.'

sauncy, lively, full of fun: 'She's a sauncy wee thing. Ye cudden keep pace with her.'

sawn, an affirmative statement, indicates that a proposal will be carried out: 'Member what they were sayin about an excursion? Sawn.'

scald, tea: 'Come on on in an we'll have a wee drap av scald.'

scalded, troubled, distressed: 'My heart's scalded with that wee lad.'

scaldy, hairless: 'The wee lad lucks terrible scaldy after gettin his hair cut.'

scrake, beginning: 'She was up at the scrake av dawn.' 'The party went on all night. We gat home at the scrake av dawn. You shudda heard the birds.'

69

scrapins, 1. Delicate, badly failed: 'She's away to scrapins. It's a pity of the woman.' 2. Left-overs: 'There's nathin in the fridge but two or three scrapins.'

scretch, wound caused by a sharp object: 'I've gotta scretch on my haun when I tried to stroke the oul cat.'

screw, grown: 'Look at the size of the wee lad, wud ye? Isn't he getting big? Screw outa all proportions.'

scringe, to grind teeth noisily: 'There I was scringin my teeth and the wife said it kep her awake.' 'The dentist said I'd scringed my teeth down till the gums.' 'I tole the wee lad nat till scringe his teeth but ye might as well talk till the wall.'

scrub, scoundrel, untrustworthy person: 'I knew from the word go that fella was a scrub.' 'He's a scrub but he gets on as if he was roilty or somethin.'

scrunch, sound made when walking on gravel: 'He was scrunchin up the garden path.'

scuff, showing signs of use: 'I tole the wee lad to watch he didden scuff his new shoes.' 'He went to Sunday school and came back with his new suit all scuffed. Ye cudden be up to them.'

scum, announces that an unexpected parcel has arrived: 'Mary, that frock you sent fer. scum.' 'John, wud ye go to the dure? It's the oil. scum.'

scunner, dislike, resent: 'I took a scunner at him after he called me names.'

scut, untrustworthy, unreliable person: 'That's a scut if ivver I saw one.' 'He's a scut of the first water.'

scuttle, Brittish Airways' Belfast-London service: 'The only way to go to London is on the scuttle.'

sedsamarley, liable to act senselessly: 'See him? Sedsamarley. Take it from me.'

sedscut, insensible, capable of foolish behaviour: 'I know the fella well. Sedscut.'

70

seeya, a parting greeting, confirms a future appointment: 'Seeya, Charlie. Orra bess.' 'Seeya Sardy.' See **seeyearoun.**

seeyearoun, a parting greeting, expressing an expectation of a future unspecified meeting: 'Cheerio fer ni. Seeyearoun.' See **seeya.**

sempy, the opposite of full: 'Luk at my glass, Alec, sempy.'

senfer, signifies a narrow or lucky escape: 'When the car whizzed past me I thought I was senfer.' 'When I swalleyed that bone I was sure I was senfer.'

sevendible, strong, sound: 'He's a sevendible wee man.'

sex, tea-time in Ballymena: 'What do you want to know what we do about sex for? Sure that's when we have our tea.'

sex mechanics, sexual offenders: 'The papers is full of sex mechanics these days. Make ye sick.' 'I've stapt buyin a paper on Sunday. Ye get nathin but sex mechanics.'

shade, 1. hair parting: 'If you wear yir bare head you'll get your shade wrecked. It's quaren windy.' 2. farmyard barn: 'He's put the ladder in the shade.'

shamrock tea, weak tea (implies it was brewed with three leaves): 'All she ivver gives ye is shamrock tea. It's like drinkin water.'

shappin, process of buying necessities: 'I'm wore out shappin.' 'Shappin's awful hard on the oul feet.'

shar, 1. shower or rain: 'That was a right bittava shar I got myself caught in.' 2. group of people, usually of doubtful character: 'The wee lad's got himself in with a right shar. One of them dyes his hair.' 'That was a right shar you were at the dance with. I wudden give one of them an inch.'

sheesahedonner, able, intelligent person: 'That one's no fool. Shees-ahedonner.' 'Sheesahedonner. That's why she was able to bate the man down to two poun from five for that sofa.'

sheugh, ditch: 'She fell intil a sheugh and she has thorns in her yit.'

Shewy, affectionate form of 'Hugh': 'I'm going to get Shewy a blazer with the initial "S" on it.' See **Quewy.**

71

shillitonme, to be attacked verbally, castigated: 'I was hardly through the door before shillitonme like a hundred of breeks.' 'I'll have to run, Harry. I'm half an hour late already. I was onny ten minutes late last night and ye shuddav seen the way shillitonme.'

shinyit, inquires if the lady of the house has returned: 'Shinyit? If she isn't I'll call back after.'

shired, cleared, refreshed: 'I want to get my head shired. I wasn't in bed till all hours.'

shizawed, indicative of eccentricity: 'Shizawed all right. Ye wudden know what she'll do next.' 'When she ast the man paintin the white lines on the road if he ever foun hisself in a corner, I said to myself, Gawd shizawed.'

shoon, footwear: 'The girl in the shop said she had a woman in an God Almighty cudden fit her feet. She said she cudden get the woman's shoon outa her head.'

shout, enquiries if the lady of the house has gone out: 'Shout? I wanted to have a wee word with her.'

shugglyshoe, shake: 'The car won't start. Cummun help me to give it a good shugglyshoe.'

shup, enquires if the lady of the house is out of bed: 'Shup yet? Mebbe I shud come back?'

shuttyer gub, shut up: 'That's what's wrong with the wumman. She won't listen when ye say to her shuttyer gub.' 'I said to her wud ye shuttyer gub and she clapsed.'

shuvaff, direction to clear off, go away: 'I tole him to shuvaff but he nivver budged.'

sickassadawg, extremely unwell: 'The wee chile gorbed herself that much at the social that she was sickassadawg.' 'Since I ate them mushrooms I've been sickassadawg. I wunner what was in them?'

sickner, disappointment, failure to come up to expectations: 'I got a right sickner when the horse came in last.' 'I got a bittava sickner when he said he was a married man.'

simmit, undervest: 'He's very cowlrife. He wears his simmit all summer.'

72

singed, clean, wash out: 'I got meers singed yesterday and I can't hear a thing.' 'Ever since I got meers singed they're givin me gippo.'

skelly, 1. glare, fixed look: 'She did nathin but skelly at me the whole night.' 2. cross-eyed: 'He has an awful skelly. The trouble was I didden know and ast him to go where he was lookin.'

skelp, blow, strike, physically chastise: 'If you don't behave I'll give you a skelp across the gub.' 'I give him a skelp and that soon brought him to his senses.'

skelph, splinter: 'I gotta skelph in my finger. It's still sower.'

skiff, light shower of rain: 'Sonnya wee skiff.'

skinnymalink, unduly thin person: 'If that wee skinnymalink hadda couple of holes in her back she'd make a right flute.'

skinnymalink meledeon legs, old-time expression of irreverence or ridicule, used by small boys concerning an elder whom they want to humiliate, esp. if the person is unduly thin: 'Ma, skinnymalink meledeon legs chased us again, so he did.'

skint, 1. penniless, broke: 'Cud ye lennus a coupla poun? I'm skint.' 2. describes intense cold: 'It wud have skint ye, it was that coul.'

skite, 1. blow with the fist: 'He give me a right skite on the face.' 2. drinking bout: 'I saw him measurin the walls. He's on the skite again.' 3. short journey: 'She tuk a wee skite down till the grocer's.' 'We went for a skite in the new car.'

skite-the-gutter, person of no account: 'Don't take any notice of him. He's onny a skite-the-gutter.'

skitter, untrustworthy, contemptible person: 'He's a skitter if ivver there was one.'

slap, gap in hedge or fence: 'I saw him abin the slap. He was stovin.'

slate, opposite of early: 'Slate. What kep ye?'

sleekit, sly, devious: 'That woman's a sleekit rat. Just you be careful.' 'She's that sleekit she wud hardly tell ye the right time.'

sleutery, limp, lifeless: 'Ye wudden take to him. He gives ye a terrible sleutery handshake.'

73

slow stamp, not express postage: 'Cud ye givvus a slow stamp for this letter? It's in no hurry.'

sluther, to drink or sup noisily: 'He drives me up the walls the way he sluthers his tea.'

sly spawn, ready-cut loaf: 'I always get a sly spawn for I fine it easier to cut.'

smallikin, beating, thrashing: 'She's lost for a good smallikin.'

smittle, infectious: 'Keep away from her. She has the 'flu and it's terrible smittle.'

sonnyme, a declaration that the speaker is alone, unaccompanied: 'Sawl rite, Sammy. Sonnyme, myself.' 'Wud ye open the dure? Sonnyme.'

sotinnit, comment indicative of hot weather: 'Sotinnit? I'm swatin.' 'Sotinnit? I'm goin to need some dorient.'

sotis, adds emphasis to a statement: 'The wire's terrible sotis. It nivver staps rainin.' '*Sardy Night Fever*'s a great picture sotis.' 'Portrush is lovely for yer hollyers sotis.'

sower, 1. painful: 'I have a sower head so I have.' 'I'm sick, sower an tired of listenin to that man yappin at me.' 2. bitter, sharp-tasting: 'That apple tart she made was that sower it wud straighten screw nails.'

spadger, sparrow: 'Wud ye luk at the darts of that wee spadger. Does ye good.'

spalterin, lame, walking unsteadily: 'There she is, spalterin down till the shap.'

spectin, pregnant. See **spittin at the tongs.**

speeley, climb with agility: 'You shudda seen him speeley up the lamp-post.'

spenser, woollen garment, knitted jacket: 'I tole him to be sure and wear his spenser or he'd be freezin, but he wudden heed me.

spitter, implies that the weather is extremely cold: 'That's a night and a half. Spitter.' 'Put some more coal on the fire there. Spitter.'

74

spittin, occasional raindrops which often precede a heavy shower: 'A minnit ago it was spittin. Now it's coming down in stair-rods.' 'This morning it was onny spittin. Now it's rainin shoemaker's knives.'

spittin at the tongs, state of pregnancy: 'Ye cud tell rightly. She's spittin at the tongs. I wonder what got intil her.'

spittin image, alike, resemble closely: 'He's the spittin image of his da.' 'Ar wee Charlotte's the spittin image of my sister's girl.'

splittin, very painful: 'My head's splittin, so it is.'

splughins, heavy boots: 'The mud'll be feet deep. Better put on yer splughins.'

spoarin, raining heavily: 'It wus onny a wee shire when I came out but luk at it ni. Spoarin.'

spoiled ratten, spoken of a child of over-indulgent parents: 'That wee lad's spoiled ratten. Luck at the way he's gettin on.'

sprachle, trip, stumble: 'He went a right sprachle intil the ditch. From the roars of him ye'd hev thought he was kilt.'

Spress, 'Daily Express': 'I like the Spress because of what it says.'

spucketin, indicates that it is raining heavily: 'This oul wire's desperit. Spucketin again.' 'Luck at it. Spucketin. That's the third time this week, and we havn't seen Tuesday yit.'

spulpin, mischievious, ill-behaved child: 'He's a right wee spulpin. He wants a good hidin.'

spurtle, tool used for thatching: 'Paddy's a quare haun with the spurtle. He can thatch like a champion.'

squarendeer, implies that a price is unduly high: 'Squarendeer to ask that much for a pair of oul gloves. I'd let my hands go barefoot before I'd pay that for them.'

stain, 1. not moving: 'Are ye stain here for a week or a fortnight?' 2. kidney complaint: 'He has a stain in his kidneys.'

stair-rods, once used to keep stair carpets in position; now an expression indicating a heavy downpour of rain: 'It was spittin at first but then it came down in stair-rods.'

75

staken dentity, erroneous identification: 'I tole the police it was a case of staken dentity but they wudden lissen.'

staken ships, popular meal: 'Staken ships fairly sets a man on his feet.' 'The staken ships ye get in Spain nivver taste the same as at home.'

stapt, ceased: 'The clack's stapt.'

stap-the-clack, someone who always expects the worst (from the custom of stopping the clock when there is a death in the house): 'Don't say a word. Here comes stap-the-clack. He'll put a dampener on everything.'

starvin, 1. suffering from extreme cold: 'I'm starvin. Put anor coupla shovelfuls on the fire there.' 2. extremely hungry: 'I'm starvin. I cud ate a horse.'

steemin, 1. raining heavily and consistently: 'You'll need your umberalla. Steemin sotis. Steemin hard.' 2. well intoxicated: 'The last time I set eyes on yer man, steemin just about describes the state he was in.'

stern, 1. mischievious, full of energy: 'The wee girl's very stern. Ye cudden be up to her.' 2. moving: 'Luck at the time it is. Eight o'clock and there's no sign of him stern. He cud sleep till doomsday.' 3. look pointedly: 'He sut stern at me the whole night.'

stikkinout, prominent, impressive, distinguished: 'That goalie was stikkinout.' 'When he gets goin on that flute of his he's stikkinout.'

stime, 1. smallest conceivable object: 'That's a terrible night. I can't see a stime.' 'Lennus a match wud ye? I just can't see a stime.' 2. a chosen moment, refers to the present: 'Stime we were on our way.' 'Stime I had something to eat.'

stocious, inebriated: 'Ack, the man's stocious again. He just can't hole his drink.'

stoonin, causing pain, painful: 'My Gawd but my corn's stoonin.' See **leppin.**

stour, dust, smoke: 'The soot came down the chimley and the stour was awful.' 'The people next dure lit a fire in their garden and ye shudda seen the stour.'

76

stovin, inebriated: 'He was as full as the Boyne. Just stovin.'

strew, honestly, in truth: 'Strew. It's not a word of a lie.' 'Strew. As Gawd's my witness.'

striffin, thin film inside an egg shell: 'She spreads the butter as thin as striffin.'

stringa misery, doleful, cheerless person: 'Ivver since he had that wet holiday he's been nathin but a stringa misery.'

strunts, displayed when ill-tempered or displeased: 'If I'd knew he took the strunts that easy I'd have give him the go by.'

stry, indicates that it is not raining: 'Thank goodness for that. Ye won't need yer raincoat. Stry.' 'Stry an it's a good job for I left my umbrella in to be restrung.'

stupa ijit, silly person: 'Ye cud sum him up in two words. Stupa ijit.' See **ijit, buckijit.**

suckey up, flatter, compliment insincerely: 'Ye needn't suckey up till me. I can see through ye.' 'Ye can suckey up there till ye're blue in the face. I'm not as green as I'm cabbage-lookin.'

sufficiency, adequate quantity: 'I'll not have another bite, thanks very much. I've had a good sufficiency.'

sughan, apron: 'Put on yer sughan an we'll do the dishes.' 'That wee wumman's a great cook. She'll be caught dead in her sughan.'

Sullen Iron, Republic of Ireland: 'He comes from Sullen Iron. Ye cud tell the minute he opens his mouth.' 'When she said to me, "Denise is six", I knew she was from Sullen Iron.'

Sunny, Sunday, the Sabbath: 'We go to wer church every Sunny morn.' 'If it's a Sunny morn he likes to spend it in his bed.'

swarm, proclamation of warm weather: 'Swarm day, I'll say that for it.' 'Swarm, an me still wearin my woolie vest.'

sweat, indicates that it is raining: 'Luck at that wire, wud ye? Sweat, as usual.'

swithers, indicates indecision: 'I'm in swithers whether I should go or not.' 'She's still in swithers about takin the job.'

77

 **tara,** terrible: 'That day's wile tara so it is.'

tare, drinking bout: 'It's terrible for her. Her man's on the tare again.' 'Harry's been on the tare for the last week. He's a turn.'

tarred, weary: 'I'm tarred out soam. I've been on the go since early morn.' 'Him? Sure if he onny strikes a match he's tarred out.'

tattie oaten, potato-bread made with oatmeal: 'A coupla farls of fried tattie oaten and he wudden call the Queen his cousin.'

tavishun, device enabling distant events to be watched on a small screen: 'He's stuck in front av the tavishun the whole night.' 'One of these days he'll be caught dead watchin tavishun.'

tea out, a restaurant meal: 'She just loves tea out when she comes up from the country.'

telt, informed: 'Mary telt me about it and so did Aggy. It must be right.'

tension, attention: 'They tole me to ring for tension but nobody came.' 'I hate that shap. They doan pay ye any tension.'

tent, small amount: 'I wunner if ye cud lennus a wee tent of sugar?'

tep, gratuity: 'Boys, shud we gie the waitress a tep?' 'If ye give the taxi man a tep wud he gie ye onny change?'

terraced, man of violence: 'I wudden go up there. You'll onny get a terraced bomb up yir backside.' 'The terraced bombs were goin aff all night.'

terrs, indicates haste: 'Ye shudda seen the terrs of him down the street.' 'The terrs of her to get to the disco—it was outa this world.'

thants, relations: 'We were up at thants for wir tea.' 'Thants want to come with us on our holidays.' 'He says he'd like to go and see thants in Tranta.'

Tharches, road junction in East Belfast: 'There's some good shaps at Tharches.' 'I offen wonder why they call them Tharches when Tharches wus knacked down years ago.'

thashes, remnants of a fire: 'They threw thee sanitary bombs in the dure and thashes wus all that wus left.'

thaveless, incompetent: 'From the luck of her I knew she was thaveless.'

thee, the number above two: 'I'll see ye outside Boots at thee.' 'The thee of us went along togerr.'

themmuns, indicates specific people: 'Themmuns is away Tittaly this year for their holidays. They do themselves awful well.' 'Themmuns an that dog of theirs. They should be in when they're out to hear the row it kicks up.'

therni, 1. recently: 'It onny happened therni.' 'I saw the two of them therni.' 2. expression of sympathy: 'Thereni, chile, you'll soon be better.'

ther thur ther, indicates close proximity: 'Are ye bline? Man dear ther thur ther, the two av them, stannin at the corner.'

thick, 1. extremely friendly, keeping company: 'Him an her's quaren thick this good while.' 2. stupid: 'Sure thon fella's as thick as champ.' 'She's as thick as two planks.'

Thingmy, person whose real name has been forgotten by the speaker: 'Mrs Thingmy was there as large as life and twice as natural.' 'I'm goin to the bingo with Mrs Thingmy. She's awful lucky.'

thissus, inquiry, often heard on a bus: 'I ast fer Chadolly Street. Thissus?'

thon, reference to a person or thing: 'Luck at the far out thon wuns is went in that wee boat.' 'Givvus a quarter of thon carmels at the enn of the shelf.'

79

thon way, pregnant: 'Charlotte's thon way again. Ye cud take yer enn at her.'

thote, the front of the neck: 'I'm away to the chemist's for some lazenges fer my sore thote.' 'She's drivin me astray in the head. One of these days I'll cut her thote so I will.'

thotherenn, the opposite portion: 'Try thotherenn, Joe. It might be asier to liff if ye try thotherenn.' 'Yir man has flitted. He's livin at thotherenn of the road ni.'

thoutfurrerado, immediately: 'Thoutfurrerado I will now present our chairman with this computer tankard as a wee momentum.'

thout veil, for sure, for certain: 'He said he'd meet me thout veil.' 'I tole you I'd be here thout veil and here am.'

thowaff, to vomit: 'Fer Gawd's sake doan start till thowaff an the flure onny washed.' 'He's a terrible man. Two or thee drinks and before ye know he'll thowaff.'

thowl, ancient: 'Thowl shoes is on their last legs.' 'Thowl coat'll do me my day.'

thrapple, throat: 'I hev an awful pain in my thrapple.' 'I onny went intil the pub to wet my thrapple.'

thrawn, awkward, unco-operative: 'He's a thrawn oul bugger.' 'She's a terrible thrawn chile. She hes me up the walls.'

throng, crowded: 'The town's awful throng this mornin.'

thundergub, noisy, persistent talker: 'Once oul thundergub starts ye can hardly hear yer ears.'

tick, heavy material: 'He shudda put on his tick vest instead of his tin wan. That's why he caught the coul.'

tile, towel: 'They thew in the tile after the secun roun.' 'Mister, I ast ye for tiles for the bathroom, not tiles for the wall. It's tiles to dry your face on I want.

tilet, comfort station: 'Mister, cud ye tellus where the tilet is?' 'I'm luckin fer the tilet. The wee lad's caught short like.'

till, not quite closed: 'Wud ye leave the dure till?'

toe-rag, unreliable person: 'Doan lissen to a word he says. He's a toe-rag of the deepest dye.'

tosh uppers, a chip shop order for two: 'Givvus tosh uppers for me and him.' 'Tosh uppers by the neck there.'

tovy, boastful: 'She'd sicken ye she's that tovy.'

trace, row of houses: 'She lives in one of them trace hices.'

tracter dacter, contractor physician: 'Thon wee tracter dacter talks awful funny. Ye'd think he was firren.'

Tranta, Toronto: 'We went to Tranta to see his bror. I didden like it. When ye get a boiled egg ye have to sup it with a wee totie spoon.'

trinket, gutteer: 'The stupa ijit drapt his piece in the trinket.'

trinnel, trundel: 'I tole him to go away an trinnel his hoop and give me a minnit's peace.'

truff, stolen articles: 'If ye ast me she has nathin but truff in the house.'

truss, have confidence in: 'I wudden truss that fella as far as I cud see him.' 'Ye cudden even truss her to feed yir budgie.' 'If theres no truss where are ye?'

tuk bad, became unwell: 'He'd be at his warm work onny he tuk bad.' 'She tuk bad in the middle of the sermon. She cudden wait till the hymn.'

tummler, a large drinking-glass: 'I hope somebody'll buy me some of them cut-glass tummlers for Christmas.' 'It's terrible when you break a good tummler. I've broke three arms myself but when ye break a tummler he gets awful annoyed.'

twaddle, nonsense: 'She just sat there talkin oul twaddel.' 'All they do at the corporation is talk a latta twaddle.'

typewriter, secretary: 'This wee girl's a shorthorn typewriter at Stormont. She gets quaren well paid.'

ulster, open sore: 'He's had an operation for an ulster on his stummick.' 'She had a terrible time with her ulster but sure she's gettin over it.'

unbenownced, unaware, unknown: 'That fella won't die unbenownced to hisself. He takes good care of Number One.' 'If that's what happened it's unbenownced to me.' 'Unbenownced to his wife he was livin in sin. Ye wudden credit it.'

unner, beneath, someone lower in grade, fewer than: 'My feet give way unner me.' 'I wudden take her unner my notice.' 'The wee lad's unner thee.'

uppity, snobbish, superior: 'I can't stann that woman she's that uppity.' 'Just because her son's a civil serpent she's that uppity ye'd think she was roilty.'

usent, formerly: 'Usent you to live in Omagh? I've seen you somewhere before.' 'Member when we usent to have proper money, not these oul dismal coins?'

 **vannal,** person who causes malicious damage: 'There was a bunch av wee vannals an ye shuda seen what they done.' 'Them vannals set the bus on fire. All they need is a good skelpin.'

venison bline man, a tradesman: 'I ast in the shap where I cud get my hauns on a venison bline man and they lucked at me as if I was away in the head.'

Venna role, a variety of bread: 'Harry's dyin about a slice of toasted Venna role.' 'I always fancy a Venna role if it's fresh.'

verbilly, by word of mouth: 'He didden tell me verbilly. He rung me up on the foam.' 'She spoke to me verbilly in the supermarket about it.'

vialin, string instrument: 'The wee lad's a quare haun with the vialin. Gawd knows who he takes it after.' 'There was a great vialin pler on the bax last night. Thon boy knew how to fiddle.'

vine, conceited: 'She's a vine wee thing.' 'I can't stann that woman. Ye wud wonder what she has to be so vine about.'

vivid, extremely angry: 'When the binmen see all them begs they'll be vivid.' 'She was vivid when she got her stackins all japped.' 'I was vivid when I foun I had walked up till my pew and me with a lather in my tights.'

wadden, cotton wool: 'I tole the chemist I wanted some wadden for meers.'

waitin on, seriously ill: 'He's been waitin on for nearly a fortnight.'

wallace, ballroom dance: 'When he ast me if I was tuk I didden know he could fairly wallace.' 'She's a great wee dancer. The way she could wallace tuk my breath away.'

wance, one time: 'I only ast him the wance.' 'We've onny been in that shop the wance.'

wanes, children: 'Now I can put my feet up and watch *Carnation Street* for the wanes is all in bed.' 'The wanes wud break yer heart but sure ye wudden be without them.' 'Wance the wains is grown up I'll have a wee bitta peace.'

wane the head, loss of reason, temporarily insane: 'Ye cud see he was wane the head when he tole the busman he wanted to go to Dallas with a loada yella man.' 'He's boun to be wane the head if he thinks he can make a livin plane the sexyfoam.'

want, lacking in wit: 'It's a pity of her. She's a noddity. She has a wee want.'

warworks, urinary organs: 'He's in a bad way. He has dodgy warworks.' 'The poor sowl's started to have trouble with his warworks. Ye cudden help but feel sarry for him.'

wattiliware, question seeking advice on choice of dress: 'We'll have to start getting ready but wattiliware?' 'If we're ever going to get to the dance I'll have to make up my mind. Wattiliware?'

wattle, a request for advice: 'Wattle I do if he doesn't turn up?' 'Wattle happen if she says she won't go?'

wed, measure, balance: 'They nivver wed the potatoes. I was flamin.' 'When they wed the bacon it wasn't what it said on the packet.'

wee message, childish mishap: 'Mister wud ye stap the bus? The wee lad's just left a wee message in his seat.'

wee softness, simpleton, slightly retarded: 'Ack am sarry for him. He has a wee softness.'

wee thing, enthusiasm, liking: 'He has a wee thing about singin. Nathin can stap him.' 'He has this wee thing about makin speeches. Ye cudden shut him up.'

well-mended, improved in health: 'After him being so bad he's awful well-mended.' 'He was awful well-mended when I saw him yesterday. He seemed to be awful glad of them grapes.'

wersh, unsalted porridge: 'It turned me when she gave me a plate of wersh.'

wettonus, request to delay, wait for the speaker: 'Wettonus, wud ye?' 'What's all the hurry. Why can't ye wettonus?'

wheeked, snatched: 'She wheeked it outa my haun.'

wheeker, exceptionally good: 'My farr's new car's a wheeker.' 'His drive from the first tee was a wheeker.' 'It was a wheeker of a match. The wee Glens deserved to win.'

wheen, an unspecified number, a quantity (large or small): 'I ast her fer a coupla spuds and she gave me a whole wheen of them.'

wheezle, chest complaint: 'He's had a wee wheezle for two or three days. He needs his chest rubbed.' 'His oul chest's actin up. Ye shud hear the wheezle he's gat.'

wherryefer, an inquiry about one's destination: 'Hello there, Sammy. Wherryefer?'

whinge, complain, whine: 'You always know he'll start to whinge if he's not enjoyin himself.' 'He'll whinge away there if he doesn't get what he wants.'

whoosthisthonis, inquiry about a previously-encountered person: 'Whoosthisthonis? That fella with the limp. I've seen him before.' 'Her in the high heels? I know her well. Whoosthisthonis?'

willicks, variety of sea snail: 'He's a great man for gatherin willicks.' 'He says there's nathin to bate a feed of willicks.'

win, current of air: 'Ye cudden hear yer ears for the win.' 'See them tyres? What I nivver had to put in them was win.'

windy, opening in the wall of a building, usually fitted with glass: 'She even gets the windy cleaner to wash the windy of her tavishun set. Didye ivver hear the like of it?'

windy stool, window sill: 'They were sittin on the windy stool hevin a wee chat.'

wire, climate: 'The wire in this place wud drive ye astray in the head.' 'This is terrible wire. It hasn't stapt rainin for four years.'

wiresawful, extreme climatic conditions: 'This wiresawful. All we can do is go home.' 'The wiresawful. We'll just take ourselves aff.'

wise up, explain, make a set of circumstances clear to someone in ignorance of the facts: 'Ach come on. It's time for you to wise up everybody about what happened.' 'I'm sittin here waitin for you to wise me up.'

wisnae, a negative statement: 'He said he'd be there but he wisnae.' 'I told him I wisnae coming and he was all cut.' 'It was a great day for the trip. There wisnae a cloud in the sky.'

worda, male parent: 'I went for a wee walk with worda.' 'Worda bought us sweeties.'

worral, capable of, able to: 'We have a new car worral do fifty to the gallon.' 'She's a chile worral do what she's told.'

wortee, evening meal: 'We usually have a fry for wortee.' 'I'm awayon. I havta go in for wortee.'

wrap, knock: 'Please wrap before leaving milk.'

wuncenferall, indication of finality: 'I'm tellin ye wuncenferall it's my last word.' 'I tole her. Wuncenferall that's the enn of it.'

wunnathem, person of a different persuasion from the speaker: 'Watch out. He might be wunnathem.' 'How was I to know he was wunnathem?' 'If he was wunnathem why didn't he say so?'

wunnenn, stand up, rise: 'Get on yer wunnenn and we'll be on our way.'
'It's about time we were goin. Get on yer wunnenn wud ye?'

wyer, whether: 'When he put it to me I tole him I was going wyer he
liked it or not.' 'How do I know wyer it's goin till rain?'

yallrite, inquiry after health or financial state: 'Yallrite again? Ye hadda bad time.' 'Yallrite ni ye've had a wee rest?' 'Yallrite? But sure ye must be, seein it's pay day.'

yap, person who is constantly complaining: 'Sure she's only an oul yap.' 'My oul woman's nathin but a natural born yap.'

yard, toilet, bathroom: 'The new house we're in is all right but it's hard gettin used to the yard bein upstairs.'

yella man, variety of candy: 'My man's like a chile. He's dyin about yella man.' 'Yella man's all right, but it's hard on the oul teeth.'

yerinfritni, a warning of danger ahead: 'Yerinfritni. Yer da's ragin mad at what ye done.' 'Yerinfritni for takin the car without astin him. Ye shudda ast.'

yer man, employer, husband, prominent politician, person whose name has been momentarily forgotten: 'Yer man was there as large as life.' 'The first fella I run intil was yer man.' 'Yer man was on the bax again last night. Every time I switch on there he is, yappin.'

yessam, an affirmation: 'Yessam goin for I promised I wud.' 'Yessam gettin up, ma.'

yilhafta, indicates necessity of a certain course of action: 'Yilhafta go or there'll be trouble.' 'Yilhafta be there on time or I'll have it in for ye.' 'Yilhafta behave yerself or we won't go.'

yin, one: 'Ma, we larned at school the day that yin an yin makes twa.' 'She's a funny yin, that new woman next door. She tole me her man cudden even drive a nail in a turmit.'

yo, female sheep: 'There's yin yo ahint the slap on her back an it canny get up.'

youse gettin, seeks to establish if a customer is being served: 'Youse gettin? If yer nat what can I do fer ye?' 'Youse gettin? What's yer complaint?'

yousens, you (plural): 'Tell yousens arwuns is ready to start.' 'Are youssens goin to Majorkey again for yer holidays?'

you stannin, challenge to one's generosity: 'You stannin, fer I'm nat? I'm skint.' 'You stannin? It's about time.'

yowtlin, infant: 'The wee yowtlin's cryin her head aff.'

yupyit, inquires whether the person addressed has risen from bed: 'Yupyit? The horns is blew.' 'Yupyit? Stime ye were on yer way.'

Z, uppermost part of the body: 'I tole him to play wayis Z.' 'If that wee centre wud onny play wayis Z we'd be on the pig's back.' 'It's a pity he lost his Z, sotis.'

zit, an inquiry, a question: 'Zit that time already.' 'Zit time I put on the pan?' 'Zit time we were on our way?'

zon, certain to happen: 'Zon all right, for I gat two stann tickets.' 'That cap I bought Sardy? Man dear, zon my head.'

John Pepper's

Ulster
Phrasebook

Illustrated by
Ralph Dobson

Foreword

It is not a happy experience, when an introduction runs, 'This is Mrs Darthy Darty. Shizza frennafmine', to discover that the lady is actually Mrs Dorothy Doherty, that she is a friend of the speaker, and that her religion is not being indicated. The aim of this phrase book of Ulster's *morr tung* is to enable such situations to be delicately avoided, to offer a guide to its infinite variations, provide a de-coder for the uninformed, and to signpost the quicksands.

It is a vernacular with many rules and a wide variety of usages, a knowledge of which will keep the unwary out of trouble. Rules, for example, which turn the town of Omagh, in Co. Tyrone, into *Omer,* transform Bellaghy into *Blahey,* and result in Clogher becoming *Clawer.* It is also made clear that if you hear someone speak of *Nora Mean* that it is the speaker's way of finding out if you know what he is getting at. Similarly, if faced with the question 'Do you like fline?', this guide will make it clear that your knowledge of cuisine is not being explored, but that an effort is being made to find out if you feel at home in an aircraft, and that the statement 'Harran Woof—they built the Tonic' is a reference to the Belfast shipyard of Harland and Wolff, builders of the ill-fated *Titanic.*

In short, students of Ulster's *morr tung* will find here an outline of some of its strangest aspects, among them many which may well be a revelation to those who consider they speak it like a native. A familiar piece of guide book advice is that it is always best to avoid behaving like a tourist. This book is designed to help the tourist to avoid speaking like one.

By Air

Ulster people are compulsive talkers when on the move. Should you get into conversation on a flight to Northern Ireland is is useful to appreciate that the way you would put things is often at variance with the manner in which the natives often express themselves.

Fonda fline?

Nathn bates a bitta crack. Wherrer ye fir?

Are you a seasoned traveller?

I feel that conversation is pleasant on a journey. What is your destination?

97

Stime we tuk aff.	Aren't we rather late?
Cud ye truss that pilate?	Is the pilot experienced?
Spumpy, innit?	Isn't it somewhat rough?
Yunna baggage ture?	Are you on a package holiday?
Nowen we lite?	What time are we due to land?
Fits ruff it'll onny start me vamitin.	I hope we have a smooth flight otherwise . . .

By Sea

How d'ye ketch the Lirpool boat?	How far would I be from the Liverpool dock?
I'm steeritch. Do we get aff last?	I am travelling steerage. Where do I go?
I hope it's a nice crossin. Ave an awful wake stummick.	I trust it will be a pleasant voyage.
I hope the scringin doesn't keep me awake.	Is it a very noisy ship?
What kine affa tip is the stuart luckin?	What gratuity does the steward expect?
A'm goanta tho aff.	I am afraid I am about to be ill.

On Arrival

Ulster people always have a friendly greeting for the visitor on the tip of their tongue. It may not always sound like one and it is helpful to be aware of this.

Formawrite?	Is the form good?
Berrinup?	Are you bearing up?
Mannijin?	Are you managing all right?
Howlinawn?	Are you holding on?
Areye ritely?	How are you doing?
Kaipinfit?	Are you in good health?

By Car

When stopping at a garage the service you get can be influenced if you use the vernacular. In many cases this can win much greater respect.

Theea thee.	I would like three gallons of three-star petrol, please.
Shuvva quarta oil intil her. She gulps one down ivvery five mints.	Put in a quart of oil, please.
A gatta pumpture.	I have a flat type.
Givvos adrappa win.	I think the pressure needs checking.
Take a wee gawk at thoil.	Would you ensure that the oil is all right?
Ave gat spension barr.	Something seems to be amiss with the suspension.
Thowl thing's nivver outa th' garritch, so it issen.	The engine is giving me a lot of trouble.

Parking

Gawd I've stapt onna double yella. Wattle ado?	Are the authorities strict about double yellow lines?
Ken farren cars park in a yella zone?	Can I park in a parking zone?
Monea visitor. Mawlrite to putt it here?	I'm a stranger. Can I park here?
Mutch d'ye hafta pay inna street ye can't get out aff?	What are the regulations about driving in a cul-de-sac?
Am a buggered onna double yella?	I presume I'm in trouble if I park on a double yellow line?
If I park here wudda run the risk of getting been up?	I'm not sure if it is quite safe to park here. Would I be attacked?

99

By Taxi

Taxi drivers are less naturally inclined to take advantage of a visitor if they are addressed in their native tongue.

Tharches as quack as ye can.
Holywood Arches, and I'm in rather a hurry.

Harran Woof's.
The Harland and Wolff shipyard.

Amgoin past Galliker's.
I want to be dropped just past Gallaher's factory.

Tharts.
The Arts Theatre.

Take us up the Ormer.
About halfway along the Ormeau Road will do me.

Durm Street okay?
Durham Street, please.

Winser Pork.
I want Windsor Park.

Hard Street.
To Howard Street, please.

Belfast's black taxis often carry a number of passengers to different destinations in the same area, rather like a bus service. Passengers usually have plenty to say to each other.

Shappins sickinin.
Going round the shops has quite exhausted me.

I havta smooth masell.
I have a great deal of ironing to do when I get home.

Yizawl heddin down the Falls?
Are you going along the Falls Road?

I'l givvera good reddin out.
I'm going to speak bluntly to my sister-in-law.

Scriminall wather astin fer a perra tights.
The price of tights is really preposterous.

The wee lad hessa bittava sturr.
My small boy suffers from a slight speech impediment.

Snivverbeenaswarm.
I cannot remember such a stiflingly hot day.

By Bus

An ability to slip into the vernacular is also valuable when travelling by bus, ensuring that other passengers do not look on you as an oddity, and therefore someone faintly suspect.

Mucher ye luckin?   How much is the fare?

Thissus?   Is this where I get off?

Wennil we get there?   How long does the journey take?

Kenna get aff ni?   Can I alight here?

Am bina season.   I would like to purchase a season ticket.

Cud ye break a fiver?   Can you change a £5 note?

Asking the Way

Should you have to ask the way it should be borne in mind that local measurements can be haphazard. This is offered as a rough and ready guide to their variations.

It's just a wee while.   40-50 yards.

Ye cud be there before yer back.   200-300 yards.

Two shakes of a lamb's tail.   500 yards.

Soney a coupla spits down the road.   Less than half a mile.

Ach it's just a wee dander.   Slightly over half a mile.

Hardly a beagle's gowl away.   Three quarters of a mile.

If ye walk fast ye'll be there in half the time.   Upwards of a mile.

Sneer a mile.   Slightly less than a mile.

Sa ferr wee distance.   Up to five miles.

101

Sa quare lick, mind ye.   Up to ten miles.

Spout ten mints afore ye cum till McFadden's pub.   A twenty minute walk.

Slat farder than you'd think.   An hour's walk.

Hotels

Hotels in Northern Ireland generally offer excellent service, but it does no harm to indicate requirements in the manner of a native.

The hate's desprit sotis.	Our room is much too warm.
The wife's friz. Cud we have more clothes on the bed?	My wife is feeling the cold. We need more blankets.
Wud ye callus atate?	Could we be called at eight o'clock?

103

We need more tiles.	We could do with more towels.
Yer a bit mangey wi' the soap.	We need a few more bars of soap.
Shire's broke.	The shower doesn't seem to be working properly.
We cud do wi' a male.	We would like to have dinner?
Wennis brakefess?	What time is breakfast?
Stable's a dead loss.	We do not like this table.
What's the dammitch?	Could we have our bill, please?
Yew trian itton?	This bill is absurd.
We onny want a drappa tay.	All we require is a pot of tea.
Ware's the wumman's classit?	Could you direct me to the ladies' toilet?

Eating and DRINKING

Eating Out

Geeusafry.	I would like fried eggs and bacon, with fried bread.
That stew wuz the quare mark.	The stew was delicious.
Put some weeten on the plate.	Could we have brown bread as well as white?
Yir pirty oaten squaren fillin.	I am told your potato oaten bread has a good reputation.
Nathin bates a vision chips supper.	Fish and chips are very tasty.

A plaita tip's outa this world.	I am very fond of fried bread.
Spotted ern wud be just the job.	Would you have potted herring on the menu?
This dush's dirty.	This plate hasn't been properly cleaned.
Ouse about some city potatoes.	We would like some French fried potatoes.
Gettus the jeez boordan biskits.	Could we have the cheese board and biscuits?
Thaddick made me turn.	I found the haddock very poor.
Good plaita parritch puts hair on your chest.	Porridge for breakfast can be quite enjoyable.
The chile just sits there pickin.	My little girl has lost her appetite.
Gaeus yin a the oot yins.	I would prefer an egg from a free-range hen.
Gaeus baked necks.	We would like bacon and eggs.

In the Bar

Yew stannin?	If you like, you could buy me a drink.
Bias a wee jar/rosiner/quick wun.	Would you care to ask me to join you in a small Scotch?
Bias a battle by the neck.	I would like a bottle of beer.
A wudden say no till a chinnan tonick.	I'll have a gin and tonic, if I may.
Howl on man or I'll go home stovin.	I really shouldn't drink any more.
A'll hevta see what a pintapour wud do till me.	I shall try a pint of porter.
Luckat m'glass. Sempy.	I'm afraid my glass needs refilling.

106

Sarry, maffit.	No, thank you very much (on being offered a drink).
Liarintilit.	Drink up.
Anor haffun and I'm away w' the Bann.	I'm afraid I have had my quota.
That fella's not only futless he's legless forby.	That chap looks a shade under the weather.
Anor glass and I'll be plastered till the gills.	One more and I'll be quite intoxicated.
Know this? A'm nicely.	I have had sufficient, thank you.
Iffa hev any more I'll be as fulasa po.	I must stop or I'll be properly under the weather.
That boy cudden bite his thum.	That chap over there is in a bad way.

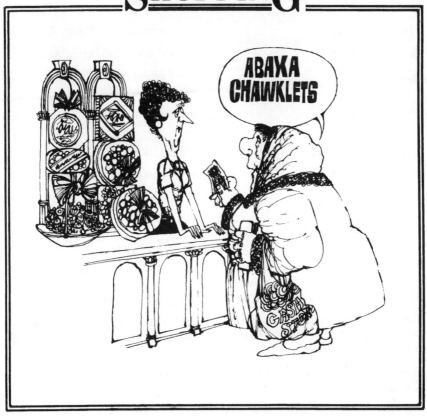

At the Post Office

Wud ye givvus a leff haun stamp?	Could I have an air mail stamp?
The stamp fell on me.	The stamp slipped through my fingers.
Sterrable what postitch costs ye ni.	Postage costs have become extremely expensive.

At the Newsagent's

Haveyea Mirr?	Do you have the *Daily Mirror?*
A'm bianamale.	I would like the *Daily Mail.*
Sixin?	Have you a Sixth Edition of the *Belfast Telegraph?*
Parshal in yit?	Has the *Impartial Reporter* arrived?
Gat the Server?	I would like the *Observer,* please.
Irsh Noose in?	Have you the *Irish News?*
New Sletterin?	Is the *News Letter* in?

In a Shoe Shop

I take sixes but I find sevens so comfortable I wear nines.	Where size is concerned I'm not really sure what fits me.
Last perr I gat here a hedda wear them for a week afore a cud put them on.	I had trouble with the last pair of shoes I bought here.
A'm luckin a perra mutton dummies.	I would like a pair of plimsolls.
I'd like a perra shoes but nat fer wearin.	I am looking for a pair of shoes for formal occasions.
The wee lad's wantin anor perra boots.	I would like a pair of shoes for the boy.

At the Corner Shop

Givvus apounna sassitches.	I would like some pork sausages.
Abaxa chawklets.	Could I have a box of chocolates?
Packitapees.	I would like a packet of peas.
Pounna shugger.	A pound of sugar.

Givvus Ferry Lickwood.	Some *Fairy Liquid*, please.
Any smoke addict?	Do you have smoked haddock?
There's a dinge in this tinna-peas.	This tin of peas is dented.
Sapoun.	The price is £1.

At the Greengrocer's

Buncha scallions.	A half-pound of spring onions.
A charra aliffs.	A jar of olives.
A pounna goosegabs.	A pound of gooseberries.
Enny carts?	Have you any carrots?
Sex orranchez.	A half-dozen oranges, please.

At the Theatre

Is there a chance affa rosiner at haff-time?	Is there time for a drink during the interval?
Themmuns is useless.	The cast is not terribly impressive.
Hev ye seen this lat makin ijits of themselves before?	Have you seen these players perform before?
That wee thing can't haff act.	The girl in the principal role seems quite talented.

At the Cinema

Any idea wire thissus an ex-pitcher?

Do you happen to know if this is an 'X' certificate film?

Wat's th' big pitcher?

Do you know what is top of the programme?

Yew seen it twyst?

Have you already seen the main attraction?

Sawrite fer th' wanes, issit?

Is the film suitable for children?

At a Party

Yew wunna them?

What religious persuasion are you?

Yer wishes granite.

Your wish is granted.

He's a grate man for the veal.

He's very dedicated, I gather. Always goes to the field for 'the Twelfth'.

Fonda willicks?

Do you like whelks?

Ye cudden bate track ruel.

I am in favour of direct rule.

He goes roun inna hunchbeck.

He drives a smart hatch-back car.

Swayafter twelve. Stime we leff.

It has got rather late.

Shizza plite wee wumman.

The lady seems to be extremely well spoken.

A ast her iffa cud liff her but she said for till ast the cisternlaw fer she was swaiten.

I asked her if she would like to dance. She said she was rather warm, but that her sister-in-law might care to.

That fella's leppin about like a hernonna griddle.

He dances with considerable agility.

A think we'll wennar way home.

I feel we should call it a day.

114

He was that boorn a cud hardly keep miseopen.	I found the gentleman somewhat boring.
John Pepper tickles me in bed every Saturday night.	I enjoy reading John Pepper's column in bed.
I split my sides at something John Pepper wrote in my bath.	I was reading John Pepper while having a bath, and found it most amusing.
My oul man puts neara pounnashugger innis tay, so he dus.	My husband puts an enormous amount of sugar in his tea.
A know ritely them battles flaff th' bekavalarry.	I have a suspicion they didn't come by that wine honestly.
When he has the drink onnim he's violin.	After a few drinks he tends to turn rather violent.
She goes allava dirr when she runs intil him.	When she meets him she seems to lose all self-control.
He keeps goin hirr an yon.	He is very restless.
He's nire one thing nor thorr.	It is difficult to assess his character.
Yer hevvin me awn.	You are pulling my leg.
Her man's ferry chalice.	Her husband is extremely jealous.
Thatwunas haughs likka churn.	The lady who has just left has a pretty sturdy pair of legs.
Dussen marr a bit.	It is quite immaterial.

At a Wedding

They went till th' waddin on their feet.

They decided to walk to the church.

Ye cud see he wus still suffern from his oul leg.

The bridegroom had a distinct limp.

That fella axas iffe wus in the peeritch.

The bridegroom carries himself well.

They're just doatin, th' perra them.

They seem to be very much in love.

He's gat awful corpulin. Ye cud say he's stikkin out.

The bridegroom could do with a little less weight.

117

Heeesa Pradessan an sheesa Cathalick.

I gather it is a mixed marriage.

In Court

He wussin playin close.

The police officer was not in uniform.

Sleegle.

It is not contrary to the law of the land.

Heesma bannister.

He is my legal representative.

Shees luckin pale.

She is seeking release on her own recognisance.

Hees gataff.

He was found not guilty and discharged.

Heesgat six. Diabalical.

Unfortunately he was found guilty and given a six month sentence.

At a Funeral

This where the dead man lives?

Is this the residence of the deceased?

The corpse's bror wants to know wattar ye hevin?

The brother of the deceased wonders if you would care for a drink.

Wud ye fancy a lift?

Would you like to be one of the pallbearers?

Whatever he died of it doesn't seem to have been anything serious.

The cause of death does not appear to have been due to complications.

118

At a Football Match

See that reff. Sed's cut.	The referee has a poor idea of the rules of the game.
Reff san ijit. Slostis bap.	The refereeing is quite disastrous.
Thon striker's futless.	The striker hasn't really shown a great degree of skill.
Arwansis fan-tastick.	Our team is playing some good football.
Themmuns can't play fer champ.	The other side's a poor lot.

119

Arwans shud get stuffed.	The home side just can't do anything right.
See that striker? Stynamite.	The striker has tremendous power.
A cud do better wi' no arms than that nit atween th' posts.	The goalkeeper is of little consequence.
Them bexis useless.	The backs are not terribly impressive.

At a Rugby Match

Yon lad plase wi' thead.	He is an intelligent player.
The full back can kick ritely.	The full back is marvellous.
That boyo's trapple croun material.	The hooker plays exceptionally well.
Gawd but yer man's futwork skrate.	His accuracy as a kicker is quite remarkable.
Why doan the forwards get stuck in?	It is time the forwards showed some enthusiasm.

At the Golf Club

Worst hole on the coorse is the fith.	The fifth hole is extremely difficult.
Ye hafta haunit till him wennies puttin.	He putts very well indeed.
Swood play's stikkin out.	He has a tremendous drive.
He's outa this world wi' a thee iron.	The man plays the three iron with great competence.

ILLNESS

At the Doctor's

Cudye get rid af this leg av mine?

I'm having considerable bother with my leg.

Ave gat this thote for thee weeks.

My throat has been painful for nearly a month.

Cud ye banditch my haun?

I would like my wrist bandaged.

Awanta git riddaf mowl stummick.

I have had fairly severe stomach pains.

Cud ye givvus anything to bring my leg to a head?

Could you give me something for my leg?

A hadda walk on m'man's arm or a wudden be here.	I would not have been able to get here without my husband's assistance.
M'man's sister's preggnan agin. Make ye spit.	Me sister-in-law is pregnant again.
Shees vines.	She is suffering from varicose veins.
Mart's awful bad.	I have a worrying pain round my heart.
Ave been bad fer neer a month.	I haven't been feeling well for some weeks.
I fell intil a sheugh and there's thorns in me yit.	I fell into a ditch and I still have thorns I cannot get rid of.
Cud a get meers singed?	I am being bothered by wax in my ears. Can I have them syringed?
Marm sproke.	My arm has been fractured.

At the Chemist's

Ma thums thobbin. Cud ye givvus somethin till stick on-nit.	My thumb is giving me a lot of trouble. A bandage might help it.
Awant catton wool for meers.	Could I have some cotton wool for my ears?
Awanta get ridda ma chest.	Have you a quick-working remedy for a chest complaint?
Mowl hed's splittin.	I have a severe headache.
I hevva bittava hursel.	I have gone hoarse.
Med's been onanaff all day.	I have a headache that keeps coming and going.
Hev ye a cure for information?	Could I have something for a slight inflammation?
Ava brust ulster.	I have an ulcer and I fear it has burst.

122

Malugs is bored so they are.

I have had my ears pierced.

Givvus a battle ferra caff.

Have you something to ease a bad cough?

A can't heer meers.

I am suffering from a slight deafness.

At the Chiropodist's

My feet's killin me.

I have walked so much that I feel quite exhausted.

You can see the pain of my bunions on my face.

I have done such a lot of walking I really need a rest.

I futted it ivvery fut aff the way.

I did not bother taking a taxi.

My wife won't be at herself till she gets her legs back.

My wife is quite worn out.

I'm aff till the chirapadist about my ingroan toe nail.

I intend to see a chiropodist about this ingrowing toe nail.

A've walked that much the ballsa ma legs is near round the front.

I am quite weary trudging round the shops.

Its that warm ma fettare like baps.

This heat has given me swollen feet.

Them patient shoos made a rite haun affma feet.

I bought a pair of patient shoes and found them most uncomfortable.

There are a number of people the visitor will never actually meet but who often stray into the conversation. It is useful to note their names, and the contexts in which they are mentioned.

Arthur Eyetis	'She has terrible arthritis.'
Billy Stain	Billy has decided not to go home.
Bridget Loan	Available at most banks.
Charlie Sin	Charlie is at home.
Gloria Site	The house has a glorious site.
Harry Soar	Harry is very annoyed.

Ivor Wun	'I for one think it is wrong.'
Mayne Yew	'Me and you both.'
Jimmy Sawn	'Jimmy's on the TV tonight.'
Ken Seer	Ken has arrived.
Maggie Sout	'Maggie isn't in.'
Nora Mean	'Know what I mean?'
Herr Tell	'I have heard.'
Jerry Spack	Jerry has returned.

Relations

Mant Nelly's a rerr tern.	I have an aunt who is quite a character.
He's the spitten image av his bror.	He is remarkably like his brother in appearance.
Kent stan th' brornlaw.	I don't get on terribly well with my brother-in-law.
The childer all take after their da. Take everything they ken lay their hauns on.	In appearance the children tend to resemble their father.
The dornlaw's nisan plite.	Our daughter-in-law is very pleasant.
Slikees farr. A ded loss.	He is rather like his father.
The farnlaw's natta bad sort.	My father-in-law is very likeable.
Ye'd think her grammar yud know better than to put gin intil her hat watter battle.	Her grandmother is full of surprises.
He's onny a haffbror.	I think he's a half-brother.
Her own mornlaw nivver shuts her bake.	Her mother-in-law is somewhat loquacious.
Th' owl man'll be here after.	My husband will be along soon.

If the owlwuman sed she wus cummin she'll be cummin.	My wife will be here directly.
Take thunkell. Spittava laff, so he is.	My uncle is good company.

Christian Names

Alec	**Ellick**
Arthur	**Arter**
Bertie	**Barty**
Billy	**Bully**
Davy	**Tavey**
Dorothy	**Darthy**
Georgie	**Jordy**
Hughie	**Shuey**
Madge	**Match**
Peter	**Peer**
Richard	**Rigid**
Robert	**Rabbit**
Willie	**Wully**
Willie John	**Wully Jawn**

Surnames

Ulster variations of common surnames are full of pitfalls. In this list the normal spelling is given first.

Bennett	**Bent**
Cahoon	**Coon**
Clarke	**Clerk**
Connolly	**Cannaly**
Crymble	**Crimmil**
Curran	**Corn**

127

Doherty	**Darty**
Donnelly	**Danly**
Douglas	**Tuglass**
Duke	**Chuke**
Falloon	**Floon**
Farren	**Farn**
Faughan	**Fawn**
Field	**Feel**
Gallaher	**Galliker**
Gamble	**Gemmel**
Gillespie	**Glespey**
Haughey	**Hawkeye**
Hewitt	**Shooit**
Lenaghan	**Lenniken**
McCullough	**McCullick**
Morrow	**Mara**
Robinson	**Rabison**
Stephenson	**Stevasin**
Thompson	**Tomsin**
Urquhart	**Urkart**
Vernon	**Vern**
Weatherup	**Wireup**
Wilkinson	**Wilkisen**

He's a born accountinant. He's grate at the figures.	He is an accountant.
Her a nacktress! Don't make me spit.	She is an actress, really?
He's no more a nectar than mowl granny.	He is surely not an actor.
Ar binmen wud waken the dead.	The binmen here are very noisy.
I leff a note for the braidman to lave four snowtaps an' a corn square.	I have left a note for the baker.

129

The wee lad lucked like a chibbley cleaner.

The young boy appeared to be a chimney sweep.

She ses she wantsa be a simple serpent.

She has ambitions to be a civil servant.

I sed she shud see a dentiss about her big mouth.

I told her she should see a dentist.

The paper put it in wrong. I'm goin till see the additer.

I intend to complain to the editor.

The lectrishan nivver came till fix th' tally.

The electrician did not repair the television.

Ar garner shudda been a plummer.

Our gardener is impossible.

He's the kine av pummlickan that shud be put behine bars.

As a publican, he runs a very poor establishment.

She's set her wee hart on bein a seeketarry.

The girl wants to become a secretary.

He earns good money for he's a fanman.

He drives a van and does very well for himself.

Ye wudden think the man was a narkiteck.

I did not know he was an architect.

130

The Time and the WEATHER

It is a common experience in Ulster, whether or not you are a stranger, to be asked for the crack time. This merely means that the questioner wants to be sure that it is as near Greenwich Mean Time as possible, otherwise the inquiry would not be made. It is useful to know how to answer.

Swun.	One o'clock.
Saff wun.	Half-past one.
Stentatoo.	Ten minutes to two.
Stoo.	Two o'clock.
Stenpastoo.	Ten minutes past two.

131

Saftoo.	Half-past two.
Thee.	Three o'clock.
Safthee.	Half-past three.
Sate.	Eight o'clock.
Saffate.	Half-past eight.
Snine.	Nine o'clock.
Sten.	Ten o'clock.
Saftenn.	Half-past ten.
Sleven.	Eleven o'clock.

The Weather

A reference to the weather is often used as a friendly greeting on a country road, to the confusion of the stranger, and it is useful to understand what the greeting really means.

Swarmwun.	It is rather a warm day.
Bravewun.	Weather conditions could be much worse.
Freesye.	That is an extremely bitter morning.
Skettinwurse.	The weather shows no signs of improving.
Sotsotis.	The weather is very warm.
Spoorwan.	Not much of a day, really.
Sardywun.	That is quite a sharp morning.
Spittinagayon.	It has started to rain.
Steeminagayon.	It has turned showery.
Scowl.	I am really feeling the cold.
Simprovin.	Weather conditions are getting better.
Warmwire.	That is a sultry sort of afternoon.

Shirey.	It looks as if there'll be showers.
Sweat.	It's raining again.
Skettinberr.	It is an improvement on yesterday.
Skeepinup.	The weather seems to be holding.
Splowy.	Isn't it stormy?
Swinnery.	That is a wintry kind of morning.
Swindy.	There is a stong breeze.
Thettinin.	It looks like rain.
Manbut thate's chranic.	My goodness but that's a terribly hot day.

Agriculture is an important part of the Ulster economy, and to a greater extent than in many other areas weather conditions are a persistent subject of comment.

Gran fer th' raipin.	The conditions are excellent for the harvest.
Mans is all japped.	My hands are chapped with the cold.
It was that cowl last night a near gat my enn.	The glass fell sharply last night.
That day wud founner ye.	My goodness but it is bitterly cold.
Hevven seen suchana wile night ferages.	The weather was as bad last night as I have experienced for a long time.
Agat caught inna shire anam ringin.	I was unlucky enough to be caught in the rain.
Stamp kine affa day.	Looks like we're in for more rain.
Stry for this timaff the year.	It has turned out dry.
Wire's gat nissen mile.	The day has turned out pleasantly mild.

133

Numbers and COLOURS

Numbers

Wan (in some areas **yin**)	One
Do	Two
Thee (in some areas **free**)	Three
Fower	Four
Fiave	Five
Sax (in some areas **sex**)	Six

Savin	Seven
Eyate	Eight
Nian	Nine
Tenn	Ten
Levan	Eleven

Colours

Vilet	Violet
Yella	Yellow
Browan	Brown
Orenje	Orange
Bludshat	Red
Cray	Grey
Wyte	White
Plew	Blue

Survival KITS

Many phrases are spoken almost exclusively in particular cities, towns and regions of the Province. The following is a sample of what you may come across in Belfast, Ballymena, and Ards.

Belfast Survival Kit

Farras a'm concerned saw-laff.

I am afraid the deal is off.

Ware's th' war works?

Could you direct me to the 'Water Works', please?

Sneer nine.

It is almost nine o'clock.

Spout seven.	It is about seven o'clock.
Mopen toffers.	I am open to offers.
A've a bror in Tranna.	I have a brother living in Toronto.
Monday was a fortnight when it happened.	It happened two weeks ago last Monday.
Sheese rite surt. Give me a glassawatter inna cup.	The lady very kindly gave me a drink of water.
A redd out ma stummick tiller.	I spoke my mind to her.
Sonny a wee plout.	It is only a light shower.
Know watta mane?	Do you understand what I'm trying to say?
She scrubbed her guts out.	As a cleaner she worked very hard.
Eesa cappen in tharmy.	He has the rank of captain in one of the top regiments.
Pity affim. He's dundan.	Unfortunately he has been made redundant.
Stussen maer.	It is quite immaterial.
Middasajeg.	My father drives a Jaguar car.

Ballymena Survival Kit

Ballymena is one area where the accent produces variations so considerable that a sharp ear and a degree of local knowledge are essential.

A dinna ken him frae Adam.	I do not know the gentleman.
He let onnis feet.	He certainly landed well.
He's that mane he wudden gie ye the time o day.	He is inordinately parsimonious.
A clapped een onner onny thorra day.	I saw her only recently.
A'd rarr hev him nor her.	I prefer him to his wife.

138

Shizza girn.	She is continually complaining.
He was on the groon, fu.	He was lying on his back.
He hut ar wee dug waya stane.	He threw a stone at our dog.
Shiz onny an owl girn.	She is extremely talkative.
A saw her abin th' cassey.	I saw her just past the forecourt.
We hev wer tay at sex.	We usually have tea around six o'clock.
Her beg wus stuffed till the gills way rubbitch.	Her handbag was absolutely crammed.
The tay's on the bile.	The tea is ready.
Givver a bowel av parritch an' she's on th' pig's beck.	She is very fond of a bowl of porridge.
He cannae dae a haun's turn ivver since he fell intil a sheugh.	He is still suffering from the time he fell into a ditch.
He cannae coont for champ.	His arithmetic is fairly indifferent.
A wus ferr deeved by the noise.	The sound deafened me.
The aul clauk disnae tell the reet time.	The clock does not appear to be quite accurate.
He's shoon wur all clabber.	His shoes were in a dreadful state.
The shap wus thrang.	The store was crowded with shoppers.
He wrot in the feels all his born days.	He has been a farmer all his life.
She giv the wee thing a quare skelp.	She hit the child a rather severe blow.

Ards Survival Kit

A canny dae.	I can do nothing about it.
A brung it hame under me oxter.	I carried it home under my arm.

139

Boat's just abin the harber. Way her heid's doon she must be haven a hunderd cran.	Our boat is about to dock. She looks as if she has at least one hundred cran of herring.
Wunna these days a'm ginnae show thon dug ma boot.	I intend to do something about their dog shortly.

In a Catastrophe

Expressions of astonishment with which to greet news of a catastrophe are well defined. Any one of the following can appropriately be used in response to any of the statements quoted, and they are freely interchangeable.

My wife has run off with the lodger.	**Yer jokin.**
Our house was burned to the ground last night.	**Awayor that.**
I've lost every penny of my redundancy money on the dogs.	**Ye don't say.**
A burgler took every penny we had when we were away on holiday.	**For goodness sake.**
The wife's having twins.	**Away to hell.**
The boy broke a leg playing rugby.	**Suffern duck.**
The wife crashed the car and it's a write-off.	**Nivver heard the like.**
I've lost my driving licence for a year.	**Cheese.**

Dialogues
TRANSLATED

In a Bar

This customer is engaged in the process of ordering a vodka and white lemonade.

'Vodkan wyte.'
'Pardon?'

'Vodkan wyte.'
'Vodka and what?'

'No, vodkan wyte.'
'Oh, white? White what?'

'Wyte lemolade.'
'What do you mean, white lemonade?
It's the only colour we have.'

'Wumman, dear there's broun.'
'Broun?'

'That's right. Broun.'
'But what on earth's broun?'

'Broun. Y'know, the colour av Scotch.'

141

In a Chippy

This customer orders fish and chips, but is told that fish is not available, nor are pies, although there are small Cornish pasties. He settles for a pasty with peas and vinegar, and goes out into the cold night.

'Fashupper.'

'Fashisaff.'

'Pysupper, then.'

'Pysesafftoo.'

'Pastiesthen?'

'Onnyweans.'

'Pastysupperthen. Annacartanapeas.'

'Vinnikeronyerpeas?'

'Aye, vinniker.'

'Scowlnite.'

'Scowlallrite.'

In a Bus

This speaker is telling a friend that he has stopped drinking and smoking during Lent.

> 'Maffit.'
>
> 'Affwat?'
>
> 'Aff thadrink.'
>
> 'Yarnat.'
>
> 'Maffthafegstoo.'
>
> 'Yamaneyer own?'
>
> 'Ivverybody's.'
>
> 'Sins wen?'
>
> 'Sins Sardy.'
>
> 'Fer wi?'
>
> 'Slent.'
>
> 'Ritenuf, affergat.'

In a Supermarket

Someone is suggesting to a friend that they might meet on Sunday. This does not suit. Tuesday is proposed but this is also unsuitable, and Thursday is suggested. Finally, Saturday is proposed, accepted and the arrangement is confirmed.

'Seeyasundi?'

'Naw, Chewsdi?'

'Thirsty mebbe?'

'Naw, Sardy?'

'Sardildo.'

'Riteyar.'

Test Your Word POWER

A simple way to test your word power is to cover up the right-hand column before checking your interpretation with the first column.

Binafleg?	Would you like to purchase a flag?
Watsit nadeaff?	What is the appeal on behalf of?
Luckatis dile.	The gentleman's face is a sight.
Heerweerstain.	We are determined to remain here.
Sannowl sayin.	It is an old proverb.
Youse plain?	Are you playing?
Senaffa nearer.	It is the end of an era.
Dozen marr.	It doesn't matter in the least.
Awanta vintitch whine.	I prefer a good wine.
He made a right hannaf ma fut.	He hurt my foot severely.
He wonna sheel at the baxin.	He is the holder of a shield for boxing.
He can sing noan.	As a vocalist he is not particularly accomplished.
Seeinasyermacusin . . .	In view of the fact that you are my cousin . . .
Seeinasyeastme . . .	In view of the fact that you were good enough to invite me along . . .
Seeinasyerafren . . .	Taking into consideration the fact that you are an old acquaintance . . .

Seeinasyerwunnafuss ...	Having regard to the fact that we share the same religious beliefs ...
Shillitonnerfeet.	She was left a handsome legacy.

A Morr Tung QUIZ

Answer the questions in this Morr Tung *fun quiz and see if you think the pitfalls of Ulster's lively vernacular would hold no terrors for you.*

1. You are at a party and someone seeking your advice draws you aside and says, 'I haven't been'. What do you say?

(a) 'Where?'
(b) 'Why, did you miss the bus?'
(c) 'Do you hope to, eventually?'

2. A woman sitting beside you on a bus says conversationally, 'I bought the chile a scribblin jarr'. What is your comment?

(a) 'That's an expensive toy, is it not?'
(b) 'Has he a sweet tooth?'
(c) 'I presume he has a literary bent, then?'

3. You are standing in a shopping queue and a woman beside you says, 'The boy has a bittava sturr'. How do you react?

(a) 'Has he defective vision?'
(b) 'He should see a doctor.'
(c) 'He should soon get over that.'

4. A woman to whom you have just been introduced says, 'See m'man? Styin about roas munn' How do you comment?

(a) 'He must have a good appetite.'
(b) 'Obviously he likes your cooking.'
(c) 'I have a weakness for it myself.'

5. You arrive at the home of your prospective host and are asked, 'Are you after your dinner?' What do you say?

(a) 'Thank you, I have already dined.'

147

(b) 'I'm not expecting it.'

(c) 'Is this an invitation to a meal?'

6. You are a guest at a party and one of the people you meet informs you, 'He's styin about samman'. What reply do you make?

    (a) 'Oh, then he's staying for some days.'

    (b) 'He is observing a Jewish festival, is he?'

    (c) 'Obviously he is extremely fond of salmon.'

7. You overhear a woman telling a friend, 'A brungerup masell'. How would you respond if this information had been addressed to you?

    (a) 'Did you indeed?'

    (b) 'You surprise me.'

    (c) 'You deserve every credit.'

8. A woman beside you in the train sees it is raining and exclaims, 'It's wet and my back's fullaf washin'. What do you say to her?

    (a) 'That's too bad.'

    (b) 'The train had better not be late, then.'

    (c) 'You obviously have a delicate back.'

9. While walking in the park a stranger, taking you to be the owner of a stray dog, says to you, 'If that dog doesn't behave I'll show it my boot'. What form does your reply take?

    (a) 'I don't think it would know much about footwear.'

    (b) 'Why, do you wear Hush Puppies?'

    (c) 'Are you out to teach it a lesson?'

Check your Score

1. *a, 0; b, 0; c, 3.*   2. *a, 0; b, 0; c, 3.*   3. *a, 0; b, 3; c, 2.*
4. *a, 3; b, 2; c, 1.*   5. *a, 3; b, 0; c, 0.*   6. *a, 0; b, 0; c, 3.*
7. *a, 0; b, 0; c, 3.*   8. *a, 3; b, 3; c, 0.*   9. *a, 0; b, 0; c, 3.*

If you scored 0-9: Be prepared for suspicious looks; 10-17: You will be labelled a stranger; 18-24: You will nearly get by, but not quite; 25 and above: You will survive with flying colours.

John Pepper's

Illustrated Encyclopedia of Ulster Knowledge

Illustrated by
Ralph Dobson

Foreword

As a rule an encyclopedia is not classified as a humorous work. This collection of facts about Northern Ireland is an exception. It seeks to show just how going shopping, buying a postage stamp, worrying about a budgie, itemising a soccer team's deficiencies, offering a cup of tea, can amusingly betray character and outlook.

Presented in these pages is a distillation of the behaviour, practices and routine described to me by a host of correspondents and those I have observed over a number of years. The tastes of the people, their lively use of language, their uniqueness and wit—all are here.

If there is a degree of emphasis on the vernacular this is because it is not really possible to provide a considered assessment of anyone without directly quoting what they have said and how they said it.

John Pepper

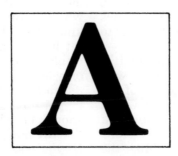

An awareness of the manner in which this letter can be ill-treated is essential for a proper appreciation of the Ulster vernacular and its eccentricities. While it is used normally in words like *pat, hat* and *mat*, it is constantly misemployed to produce *gat* for *got, hat* for *hot, lat* for *lot,* and *rat* for *rot,* as in 'that's a ratten oul day'. *Shap* is heard when *shop* is intended and *doctor* is transmuted into *dacter.*

Anyone named Scott will be addressed as *Mr Scatt.* It may turn Mr Scott blue in the face but there is nothing he can do about it. He is as helpless as Mr Potter who has to recognise that many people refer to him as *Mr Patter.* A dish of porridge will be *a plate aff parritch.*

A holidaymaker sun-bathing on the beach at Portrush with his daughter heard a jazz programme on a nearby transistor, suddenly recognised one of the tunes, and said, 'That's Nat King Cole'. Immediately the girl asked, 'Who is it then?'

A Belfastwoman told a friend, 'It was that hat my husband left aff his simmet'. A different note was struck when a newly-appointed hospital matron asked a patient how he was feeling. 'Ach, I'm not so hat,' he replied, indicating that he could have been better. She turned to a nurse and said, 'Get this man another blanket.'

ABYSS Approximates to the divide which distinguishes the working-class Ulsterman from those who consider themselves 'upper-class types'. The UCT can usually be identified by their shrewdness, a frequent tendency to be avaricious, the fact that they rarely wear a hat, dislike *Coronation Street*, are not regular church-goers, are enthusiastic about golf, squash, bridge and rugby, and sometimes *Match of the Day.* They would restore hanging, are mad when they read of the activities of people like Arthur Scargill, have no interest in pub darts, drink gin and tonic, 'Black Bush', or Bacardi and Coke, insist on their daughters having piano lessons, and usually have a stock of stories which they sometimes tend not to tell too well.

They are particularly fond of Ballymena stories and will simulate the accent to tell of the defence witness in a case in which a man was charged with injuring a neighbour by throwing a stone at him. Seeking to establish the size of the missile counsel asked, 'Was it as big as your fist?' 'It was bigger.' 'Was it as large as your head then?' 'It was bigger but it was nae as big as yours.'

As an encore there might be the story of the man conducting his own defence who was told, 'You may challenge any member of the jury now being called.' 'Right,' he replied, 'I'll fight that wee cross-eyed mon fornest ye.'

The average UCT tends to refer to himself as 'yours truly', and will frequently address you as 'Squire'. Likes starting statements with 'actually', has never been to a wake in his life, and is fond of sailing.

Will have days of quiet amusement thinking about it after being told of the Belfast boxer who said of an opponent, 'He'll give me no bother. He has an Achilles' heel. It's his jaw. It's made of glass.'

ADVICE When this is sought it is advisable to be aware of certain conventions. If you are approached by a native his inquiry will often sound rather more like a chal-lenge, as in, 'You don't know where Durm Street is?'; 'You don't know the right time?'; 'You would-n't have a match on you?'; 'You wouldn't have change of a poun on you?'

Similarly if you seek guidance to get to your destination you should be prepared for answers that are not quite straightforward. If you ask where a particular street might be you are apt to be told, 'Keep on the way you're going and you'll know it by the wriggly tin', in other words, by the corrugated iron fencing.

A motorist in Co. Londonderry who lost his way was advised, 'Ye'll hae to turn the car rount and go on down to the bottom of the hill there and take the road that lies till your left haun. Then if you don't lose the bap ye'll get there soon enough.'

Another motorist was left none the wiser when told, 'Keep on down the road and watch out on the right till you come to a big cheeser tree a couple of spits from Brannigan's pub where you'll see a big wide road. Don't go down it. The road you want is away past that on the left. Just ask anybody.'

AFTERNOON It is useful to know that this is a time of day rarely spoken of. Whereas else-where it is usually taken to mean the period between two and six o'clock p.m., this is generally referred to as evening in Ulster. In

152

England, 'long winter evenings' will be mentioned. In Ulster it is 'short winter evenings and long winter nights'.

ANSWERS There is much evidence of a tendency to avoid a direct 'yes' or 'no' when anyone is asked a question. People will feel awkward not so much because a straight question is put to them but rather by reason of their resentment at being forced to give a reply. A stranger who seeks to make sure he is on the right road for a bus station will never be given instant confirmation. Rather he will be asked in turn what is his destination and why, where he came from, did he enjoy himself, does he have any family. Finally, curiosity satisfied, the information he seeks will be provided.

When the question is inane the inclination to use irony in reply is rarely resisted:

'Haven't I seen your face before?' 'Probably, I've had it a long time.'

'Your head's bandaged. Did you get hurt?' 'I have a headache and the chemist asked me to try this as he was out of aspirins.'

'Are you limping?' 'No, this is a new dance step I picked up.'

'That's a nice tan. Are you back from your holidays?' 'You could be right. I thought this place looked familiar.'

'Somebody said your wife had left you. Has she?' 'No she's just gone to the Isle of Man for a fortnight with the windy cleaner. I'm on the pig's back.'

ANTRIM, COUNTY (pop. 352,549) A county in which the influence of the Scottish Presbyterian settlers is still strong. Pipe band music has a considerable following although this cannot be said of the kilt.

A mother commented to a neighbour, 'The wean went oot to school this mornin greetin buckets.' Clearly the child was not a dedicated scholar.

A caller at a North Antrim farm was told by the woman of the house, 'Come on on in an see the boss lyin on the sofa spillin his breath.' He was having a sleep.

On one of the rare occasions when Lough Neagh was frozen a villager said, 'If a hadda knew the Lough was friz ah'd have went to have saw it.'

When the inexorable happens the comment will be made, 'It betabe', and if someone says, 'twarthy', they mean two or three.

A gardener, bothered by the havoc caused by wood pigeons on his broad beans, asked in a pet shop for a 'board net to stop the boards from aitin my bains'.

A small boy who found a dead owl took it to his mother, who shouted, 'Take that oul ool oot o' here.'

A herd of cattle will usually be described as, 'A clatter o' bastes.'

A shopper, when told the price of an article was £1.10 said, 'I'm sure you'll throw off the 10p.'

153

'Missus,' he said. 'If I could throw off 10ps I'd be in the kitchen w' my heed ower the sink.'

County Antrim people know when it is St Andrew's Day and Burns' Night but they will not normally be adept at throwing the caber.

A party of German tourists travelling by bus stopped briefly in Ballyclare where they visited a local cafe. A resident, asked afterwards what he thought of them, said, 'A hevney muckle opinion about any yin thet disney speak the same as werselves.'

ARSE Slang, all-purpose term generally avoided by the middle-class, who will refer to the 'rear end', sometimes 'the posterior' or 'the bottom'.

A woman, grumbling at the difficulty of keeping her small son neatly clothed, said, 'I bought him a pair of trousers and he had the arse outa both knees before you could say Jack Robinson.'

A short distance will be covered by, 'It's not a kick in the arse down the road', and someone who walks aimlessly around will be summed up by 'All he does is arse about', or, 'He's never done arsin' about the lawn.'

A man who slipped and fell declared, 'I lit on my arse', while a decision to take no action will be conveyed by, 'I didn't bother my arse.'

A bore will be 'A pain in the arse', and, 'Arse about face' is another way of saying 'back to front.'

(see BEHINE)

154

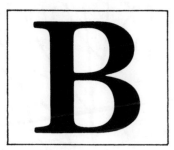

BACK Normally this means the rear of the house, as in, 'They broke into my back', although a query at the grocer's, 'What's your back like?' betokens an anxiety to find out if the bacon can be recommended.

'He lives up my back', shows that the back of the speaker's house is in close proximity to his own.

'Back up' is an instruction to a horse to reverse. 'Back away there' directs the animal to continue to do so. 'To back a horse' is another matter and specifies that money has been placed on the animal in the hope of a considerable financial return.

A hairdresser asked a customer, 'Do you want your hair cut down the back?' He replied, 'Isn't there enough room where we are?'

A man who grumbled, 'The wife's never aff my back', merely echoed a common whinge.

BALLYMENA Co. Antrim (pop. 55,000). Sometimes called 'Disneyland' because of the constant references to it heard there, as in, 'The child disney like her breakfast', 'My man disney like Tap Aff th' Paps. Says it sickens him', 'I asked the wife to come for a walk but she disney want to.'

The idiom embraces such verbal peculiarities as, 'We'll go down to the chinky for a snake', otherwise a light meal at the Chinese takeaway. Also to be heard is, 'He's a quack doctor', indicating that the speaker's general practitioner makes his decisions quickly, not that the man is unqualified.

'I spoke to the head yin', implies a discussion with the boss.

Ballymena is a paradise for anyone interested in *quent speech*, i.e. the quaint use of English. Much of it is of Scottish origin, thus giving rise to the town's reputation for prudence. There is, however, no justification for the suggestion that the statement, 'I shook hands with a friendly Arab. I still have my hand to prove it', could equally have been said of a Ballymena man.

The natives are kind-hearted and hard-headed, devout, concerned with what the neighbours think about them, but insist on value for money.

The man who complained about the soda farls bought in a home bakery, 'Them boys is stale. Them boys is yesterday's,' was merely standing up for his rights, demonstrating, 'You hae the wrang soo by the lug this time.'

In the rich farmlands surrounding the town people will speak of 'having a coo or two', indicating possession of a formidable herd of valuable cattle. 'A wee bit of land' could embrace anything up to 200 acres. 'That's a fine yo' connotes a first class ewe 'worth a bit of money'. A stockbroker is a dealer in 'stocks and shears'. A woman shopper who asked for 'curn jam without curns in it' was seeking blackcurrant jelly.

BANAGHER Banagher Glen in the Roe Valley has an old parish churchyard in which an ancient Irish saint, St Muirdeagh, is supposedly buried. Sand from the grave is considered to have magical properties in warding off misfortune on the grounds that 'the sand of Banagher bates the divil.'

A reputed cure for a cow which has stopped giving milk is to wrap a leaf of the Bible containing a small quantity of Banagher sand round its horn. It was the answer to the milk blinker, someone able to cast a spell on a milking cow.

To declare, 'That bates Banagher and Banagher bates the devil', is to indicate astonishment at a happening or an argument.

To say of a comic 'That fella bates Banagher', points to his excellence as an entertainer.

BAX This has become the equivalent of an altar in the home. It holds all ages and all sexes in its grip, the worship starting at an early hour and lasting until after midnight.

The Belfastwoman who said, 'My oul lad clacks in front of the bax all night', was not describing someone out of the ordinary.

There are other meanings for the word, however. A woman will say, 'When our Jimmy goes aff till his work ye can see the wee bax strapped on the back of his bike for his samwitches.' In the same vein is, 'The oul lad has a wee plastic bax for his piece. A blue one.'

There is a different meaning in 'I gave the wee lad a bax on the ear.' The message here is that he has been misbehaving.

There is a common weakness for putting people 'in their bax'. It conveys a minor triumph as in 'I gave her a piece of my mind. That put her in her bax all right.'

BEHINE Uttered with special emphasis on the last syllable, this is the equivalent of the French *derrière*, and the English *backside*.

A woman will say admiringly of her baby grand-daughter, 'She has her mother's behine.'

The expression figures in such statements as, 'He give me a dunt and I landed on my behine in the trinket', and, 'That lad wasn't behine the dure when the brains were given out.'

Other variants include, 'When that woman plants her behine in your house ye may say goodbye to Carnation Street,' and 'That's a quare wet day. A day like that and ye cud be gutters up to the behine.'

It was used during a shopping expedition by a Co. Tyrone man in search of a china dog for his mantelpiece. 'It fell and got broke,' he explained. 'Do you want a right-hand dog or a left-hand one?' he was asked. 'I don't rightly know,' he replied. 'All I can tell you its behine points straight down the main street in Portglenone.'

The comment was made of a man of unduly small stature: 'His behine should have a sweet enough smell, for it's brave and near the daisies.'

Said of a girl on becoming engaged to a man considered by the speaker to be of poor character: 'If that poor girl has burned her behine, it's her who'll have to sit

157

on the blisters.'
  (see ARSE)

BELFAST (pop. 305,600). City of contradictions, statues and strong convictions. The rows of kitchen houses are gradually being replaced by more attractive homes whose tenants are apt to explain, 'the yard's upstairs', a tribute to the fact that there is no outside toilet.

Ulster poet Bill Nesbitt wrote these lines about it in 1968 and finds them still regularly quoted, constantly in demand. They were read on an Ulster radio programme and the BBC sent more than 800 copies to listeners who wrote asking for them:*

> I'll speak to you of Belfast, stranger, if you want to know,
> So listen, and I'll tell you why I love this city so...
>
> BELFAST... is an Ulsterman, with features dour and grim,
> It's a pint of creamy porter, a Sunday morning hymn,
> A steaming pasty supper, or vinegar with peas,
> A little grimy café where they'll serve you 'farmhouse' teas,
> A banner on July the Twelfth, a sticky toffee apple,
> An ancient little Gospel Hall, a Roman Catholic chapel,
> A *Telly* boy with dirty face, a slice of apple tart,
> A fry upon a Saturday, hot 'coalbreek' on a cart,
> A Corporation gas-man, complete with bowler hat,
> A wee shop on a corner with a friendly bit of chat,
> An oul' lad in a duncher, a woman in a shawl,
> A pinch of snuff, a tatie farl, a loyal Orange Hall,
> A tobacco smell in York Street, a bag of 'yella man',
> An Easter egg that's dyed in whin, a slice of Ormo pan,
> A youngster with some spricklybegs inside a wee jam-jar,
> A meeting at the Custom House, an old Victorian bar,
> Mud-banks on the Lagan when the tide is running low,
> A man collecting 'refuse', bonfires in Sandy Row,
> A bag of salty dullis, a bowl of Irish stew,
> And goldfish down in Gresham Street, a preacher at a queue,
> A portrait of King Billy upon a gable wall,
> A flower-seller on a stool outside the City Hall,
> A half-moon round a doorstep, a 'polisman' on guard,
> A pedlar crying 'Delph for Regs!', a little whitewashed yard...
>
> And there's your answer, stranger, and now I'm sure you'll see
> Why Belfast is the only place in all the world for me.

It will never dawn on a Belfastwoman who tells her husband, 'I saw Mrs McCluggage coming through the window', that she might be taken literally. Nor are the words, 'That left fut of the wife's isn't near right yit', considered ambivalent.

Two nuns passed a Belfast woman and her small son in a Dublin street. The boy asked,

* Reproduced by permission of the author.

'What d'ye call them, ma?' 'For Gawd's sake,' she rebuked him, 'houl yer tongue or they'll know we're not one of them.'

A Belfastman whose house suffered severe flooding told a friend, 'It was terrible. I was just in time to save a soda farl from going down a third time.'

An East Belfast woman angrily told her small son as he was about to dash across a busy street, 'Come here this minute. D'ye want to get yerself kilt like they advertise on TV?'

Also typical was the comment of the woman whose husband was papering a room with wallpaper that had a complicated pattern of ducks and geese. When she arrived to inspect the finished job the floor was littered with left-over pieces. 'Man dear,' she exclaimed. 'Ye hev enough ducks and geese left to keep us in broth for a month.'

Usually pronounced *Bēlfast*, with the accent on the first syllable, but experts insist it should be *Belfāst*, with the accent on the second.

BIRTH Friends will say of a pregnant woman, 'She's thon way.' This is a condition which gave rise to the inquiry, 'Do I have to be seduced to be able to claim infertility benefit?'

Another pregnant patient queried anxiously, 'Will I have to have a sectarian birth?'

Of a mother with a child born out of wedlock it will be said, 'She's not married. She just had it.'

BIT This figures persistently in Ulster speech. Rather than announce the purchase of a new overcoat a Co. Antrim man will say, 'I bought myself a bit of an oul coat.'

A Co. Tyrone speaker will 'take a bit of a look at a new car,' and refer to a young woman as 'a bit of a girl'. 'A bit of a night' means one marked by much jollification.

Approval will be indicated by the statement, 'It's a bit of all right.'

Other usages include, 'He's a bit of an ijit', 'I'm going for a bit of a walk', and 'I gave her a bit of my mind.'

The statement, 'It's a bit down the road', can mean anything from one mile to five.

A person who says 'not a bit of it' is indicating violent disagreement with whatever opinion was put to him.

BLESSINGS While a blessing is the least expensive way of indicating appreciation this is no reflection on the sincerity and colour which generally goes with one. If blessings are going out of fashion it is because they can often be so fulsome and suspiciously flowery as to embarrass the recipient. 'May the devil never hear of your death till you're safe inside the gates of heaven', and, 'May every hair of your head turn into candles to light your way to paradise', would make most people squirm.

Today's blessings avoid the unctuous and run to the familiar, 'May your shadow never grow less', or 'May you be dead a year before the devil hears about it.' Satanic allusions, however, are going out of fashion.

Much depends on the reason for this style of expressing goodwill; whether, for example, it voices gratitude for a loan, a wage increase, or the provision of a drink when dying of thirst. 'May God put a strong thatch on that head of yours', and, 'May a doctor never earn a pound aff ye,' are acceptable but not really taken seriously. There are still followers in country districts of 'May the wind be always at your back', and 'May you rest in piece but not in pieces.' Dated blessings are, 'May you live that long that the skin of a gooseberry would make a skirt for you with seven flounces in it', and 'May you live till a goose-gab skin makes you a nightcap.'

A modern businessman would have some other device for wishing his obliging bank manager well than by saying, 'May misfortune follow you all your days and never catch up with you.' It would be more realistic to explain, 'May your giving hand never wither.'

BREADMAN The man who delivers the bread is as traditional a figure in domestic life as the milkman. As in a home bakery, he may have on offer an infinite variety of delicacies, from a 'sore head' to 'a flies' cemetery', a 'sliced pan' to 'gravy rings'.

In some areas a request for a 'duck's neb' will mean that a Vienna roll is wanted. An order for a 'fresh lodger' indicates that a cylinder-shaped loaf marked off in half-inch slices is sought.

A well-stocked bread-van will carry soda and wheaten farls, crusties, fadge (otherwise potato farls), sliced pans, rolls, and pious buns.

A competitor in a bakery contest who failed to win a prize for his sodas was told that two of the three judges were from England. 'What wud ye expect,' he protested indignantly. 'What wud a coupla ijits of foreigners know about sodas?'

In many households this saying is still looked on as Gospel: 'Ate the crusts. They'll make you wise', which implies that they are conducive to frugality and thrift.

BUTCHER A trader who needs to have his wits about him to cope with sharp-tongued customers. His shop is a popular platform for pointed comment.

A boy returning a pound of steak said, 'My da says he could sole his boots with that.' The butcher sourly asked, 'Why didn't he then?' and was told, 'Sure he cudden get the nails through it.'

In a case where tripe was in little demand a customer was persuaded to give it a trial. Later, when asked how she liked it, she said, 'To tell you the truth my heart didn't lie to it so I gave it to the dog.' The outraged trader replied, 'Don't tell me he turned up his nose at it as well.'

A Newtownards butcher, when given an order for a sheep's head, was told, 'Leave the eyes in to see us over the weekend.'

In a village butcher's a customer remarked, 'Isn't it just beautiful here. Some day I would just love to be laid to rest in the nice wee churchyard down the road there.' Politely the butcher said, 'You'll be very welcome I'm sure, missus. We'll give you a funeral you'll never forget.'

If a customer says, 'My man's dead nuts for rose munn', a butcher will know instantly that her husband is a roast mutton buff.

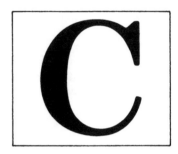

C

CAP Chiefly but not exclusively male headgear, sometimes known as a duncher. It has been hit by the vogue for bare heads.

Caps come in various styles. There are those which can be folded and kept in the pocket when the occasion demands, and others of more formal design suitable for a hallstand or hanging in a cloakroom.

A definition of a gentleman runs, 'He hangs his cap on the hallstand. He doesn't sit on it.'

One style inspired the comment 'That fella's cap lucks like a landin' pad for pigeons.'

There are men who wear their caps inside the house as well as out. A bareheaded Belfastman encountered on a pouring day was asked why he wasn't wearing one and said, 'Sure I came into town to buy myself a new one.' To the inquiry, 'But why aren't you wearing it then?' he answered, 'Sure I cudden sit around the house in a wet cap.'

A compliment is intended when it is said of a person, 'If you were in trouble he'd think nathin of puttin his cap roun for ye.'

A woman in an Armagh supermarket was heard to say, 'My husband went out without his cap and the wine was that fierce he came home with his head blown aff him.'

A woman who had a small boy by the hand asked in a hat shop, 'Can I have a cap to fit the wee fella? He has a square-shaped head like his da but if a round cap fits him I'll just take it.'

CHARACTERS These are in plentiful supply even if the comment is constantly heard, 'There aren't so many characters these days.' Every district has its own examples.

Down the years Belfast has produced 'Happy Jimmy', who toured the streets playing hymns on a hurdy-gurdy; 'Forty coats', so called because he went out with at least four or five ragged coats to keep him warm; 'Cowboy Joe', who cycled round the streets wearing a stetson, and riding as if his mount was a Wild West horse; and 'Choke the ducks', a religious oddity who roamed the city centre, with a Bible under his arm, and whose response to the jeers of small boys was to kneel on the pavement and pray for his tormentors.

CHEMIST Someone expected to provide a cure for almost every known ailment or complaint on demand. Besides his professional qualifications, if he is to stay in business, he must have a sound knowledge of the idiom and its peculiarities.

He will cope with ease with such requests as, 'The oul lad's corns is stoonin. Cud ye givvus some of them plasters to shut his gub?'

He will be unfazed by the customer whose age was asked for and who retorted, 'Dammit man, it's a rub I'm after, not a death certificate.'

Nor will he be troubled by the request, 'Wud ye send it down? It's my feet, y'know.'

It is all part of his day's work behind the counter to be faced with the complaint, 'The tablets you said would put me back on my feet musta been the wrong ones for they've done nathin' but make me run to the back.'

Probably apocryphal is the story of the chemist who handed a customer a bottle with the words, 'If this doesn't work, come back and I'll have another go at making out the doctor's handwriting.'

A Co. Antrim chemist was told, 'I want something to worm a dog.' He produced a hot-water bottle.

'Are ye mad?' he was asked. 'The wee thing has worms. I want something to worm the poor animal.'

A Belfast woman who went into a Boots store in London and asked for some headache powders was handed a packet of sanitary towels.

A Tyrone chemist was asked, 'Could you give me something for my arm. It's that sore I haven't been able to put on me for a week.'

CHERRYVALLEY Belfast suburb associated with ostentatious speech, due mainly to the way in which Belfast comedian James Young used it as a vehicle for poking fun at people who spoke with a marble in their mouth. He would refer to it as 'Cherryvelley', where the residents got their 'herr done' and would ask for 'sperr ribs' in a Chinese restaurant. They would say 'the weather's ferr', declare they 'wouldn't derr' go to see a dirty film, and speak of 'going upsterrs'. They would buy 'a new perr of shoes', say 'I don't kerr very much for an omelette', and describe an acquaintance as 'a rerr type.'

In fact, the residents of Cherryvalley have every reason to be resentful of the reputation given them, and to insist that it is 'quite unferr'.

CHILDREN The new generation is an unpredictable and amusing as those in any other part of

Britain. At school they display the usual tendency to take things literally, with unexpected results.

A teacher was explaining to her class the uses of the different senses. A little girl who had chattered incesantly was given the order, 'Hold your tongue.' The teacher then went on to ask, 'What do we have noses for?' From another pupil came the answer, 'To wipe, sir.' It was then seen that the first child was sitting solemnly holding her extended tongue between her fingers.

A boy not long at school was going over, at home, the words he had been taught. His father, however, kept correcting him until the child finally burst out, 'You're trying to make an Egypt out of me, aren't you?' Dad had no answer.

Another new pupil arrived home to announce, 'A lady had twins on the bus.' To the startled inquiry, 'And what happened?' he replied, 'She was taking them to school.' He had the same gift for the unexpected as the boy who broke the lead in his pencil and called out, 'Miss, the wick has gone down.'

A youngster who wasn't at all musical was told to leave the singing class and join another group. Next morning his angry mother arrived, demanding an explanation. The teacher pointed out, 'I'm sorry but your son just doesn't have an ear for music.' Protested the mother: 'If that's the case sure he has a lug like a saucer.'

Although marital status is not usually associated with geography a boy whose task was to write what he had learned about two American rivers obediently penned: 'They are Mrs Sippi and Miss Souri.'

A five-year-old boy arrived home from school in tears and explained that teacher had asked all those who wanted to go to heaven to raise their hands. 'You raised yours, didn't you?' his mother inquired. 'No,' sobbed the boy. 'Sure you told me to come straight home.'

At a kindergarten party one little boy said he had been absent from school because his mother had been away to 'bring home a new babby' and he had returned specially for the party. When it was sought to find out if the new arrival was a boy or a girl he looked puzzled, did not answer, and trotted off, but was waiting at the door when the teacher was leaving. Tugging her to one side he said confidentially, 'I don't know if it's a boy or a girl. They say it's a thing called a sister.'

Religious instruction is a minefield for curious, bewildered young minds.

In a Co. Antrim school in an area with a wide following for horse jumping there had been a lesson on the story of the ten lepers. 'Why did the lepers stand afar off?' the question was put. The answer came unhesitatingly, 'To get a good run for their lep.'

When one class was asked, 'What did the angel Gabriel say to

Mary?' it brought the suggestion, 'Hello, Mary. You're going to have a ba.'

A boy who was faced with the need to read a passage from St John starting, 'In the beginning was the word...' started off perfectly, but when he came to the next sentence he read, 'There was a man sent,' then paused before resuming, 'By God, his name was John.' He was sternly warned to mind his stops and commas in future.

One child, tested by his mother to find out what he had learned, said, 'It was about God sending Moses to rescue the Israelites from the Egyptians.' It was suggested he should tell her the details. He replied, 'She told me that when the Israelites reached the Red Sea Moses built a bridge and the Israelites trooped across before they could be hemmed in by the enemy tanks. Then when they all got across the bombers blew up the bridge.' Astonished, the parent demanded, 'Did the teacher actually tell you that?' With a shrug the boy replied, 'Gosh no, mum. If I told it to you her way you'd never believe it.'

Confronted with the query, 'What did Isaac do in the Bible?' a pupil said, 'He worked on the roads.' The embarrassed teacher later discovered that the lad's father, also called Isaac, was a road worker.

During an elementary lesson on geography at a primary school the nun who was teaching gave some facts about the Irish climate. She turned a blind eye to the normal damp weather conditions and tried to convince the class that in Ireland the sun always shone, saying, 'In summer it is very hot here.' She was left speechless by a retort from the back of her class, 'Aye, sister, and the sky gets so hot that it nearly always sweats.'

It became a matter of routine with a perpetual latecomer to call him before the class, ask his excuse, and an automatic caution would be delivered. One morning he was unusually late and was asked: 'What's the excuse this time?' He replied, 'The Council's laying a pipe-line along our road and they've dug a hole at the end of our lane. During the night a horse fell into it and they couldn't get it out. I had to wait till they shot it before I could get across.' Sceptically the teacher inquired, 'And did they shoot it in the hole?' Replied the boy, 'No, sir. They shot it in the head.'

In one home gramps was fond of constantly reminding his grandson about the changes in school life since he was a pupil. 'We had to do all our exercises on the slates,' he pointed out. 'Weren't you afraid of falling?' came the query. 'What do you mean?' asked gramps. 'Sure you said you did all your exercises on the slates,' persisted the child.

CLERICS There is a strong and intimate relationship between clergy and people. In rural areas a clerical visit is an occasion.

A young curate visiting an ailing member of his congregation told her, 'I'm pleased to see you do not repine at the sufferings providence has put upon you.' She replied, 'My rheumatism is bad indeed but I still thank heaven I have a back to have it on.'

A worshipper decided to go to church after a long absence and dressed specially for the occasion. The feathers in her hat were being tossed by the draught from a nearby window. The minister paused on his way down the aisle to welcome her and inquired if the wind was bothering her. 'It's all right,' she answered. 'I'll overcome that when the organ starts.'

A former vicar and his wife decided to attend a social in his old parish. 'I'm delighted to see you,' said his successor. 'And is this your most charming wife.' Quietly came the answer, 'This is my only wife.'

A Sunday school teacher, determined that her class would do well in an examination by the minister, rehearsed them carefully. Each was to be asked a question from the Shorter Catechism, starting with, 'Who made you?' 'God.' 'Of what are you made?' 'The dust of the earth', and so on. On examination day, as the class waited, the first boy asked if he could 'leave the room', and was still absent when the questioning began. The second boy was asked the first question:

'Who made you?' when he replied, 'The dust of the earth' he was told 'No, son. God made you.' Said the boy, 'You're wrong, sir. The wee lad God made is out in the toilet.'

A visiting minister enjoined a member of the congregation full of complaints, 'Always remember the good book tells us to be content with our lot.' Replied the man, 'That's the trouble. I haven't got a lot.'

A Roman Catholic priest encountered a party from the village who had been to an Orange demonstration. All were in good spirits. 'Did you have a good day?' he asked them good-humouredly. 'We did indeed,' came the answer. 'We had the time of our lives kicking the Pope up and down the field.' The cleric smiled and said, 'Well, it just served him right. He shouldn't have been there.'

A veteran member of a golf club with a reputation for lurid language was introduced to a visitor seeking a round, named Dr Abernethy. The visitor proved much the better player, the veteran as a result becoming progressively worse. With the game on the verge of being lost, the veteran found himself in one of the club's most notorious bunkers. As he studied his lie he called to his opponent, 'Doctor, before I play this shot—tell me, are you a DD or an MD?'

Among a Co. Down dean's unforgettable visitations was one where he had knelt to lead a parishioner and his wife in prayer.

166

A moment later their young son rushed in from the street in a cowboy hat, jumped astride the dean's back, and cried out happily, 'Gee up there.'

A Co. Antrim minister, learning that one of his flock was ill, told the man's wife that he would call to see him. 'But he mightn't know you, for he is randerin,' she pointed out. The cleric said he would call anyway and next day made the journey through snow and mud to a lonely farm at the back of Slemish. 'You came after all,' said the wife. 'I'm still feared he mightn't recognise you for he's still randerin.' However she led him into the bedroom where she announced, 'Now, John, who is this with me?' The man looked up. 'That's the Reverend John James Gilmore, the best and finest wee meenister we've had for a lang time,' he said firmly. The wife gave the minister a look. 'I told you he was randerin, Mr Gilmore,' she said.

CONVERSATION Dialogue, whatever the circumstances, can reach considerable heights of complication.

A man telephoned a tourist office and asked the cost of a room at a Ballycastle hotel and was told, 'Sorry. Our brochure with the details is not out yet.'
'When do you expect it?'
'I don't really know.'
'The hotel isn't in the 'phone book. Do you think I should 'phone Directory Inquiries?'
'I don't know.'
'You don't mind me asking these questions.' 'Not at all. That is what we're here for. If you don't ask you'll never know.'

On rather similar lines was the conversation between a passenger and a man in the ticket office at a rail station.
'Can I get a train here?' the passenger asked.
'I don't know about that. You can get a ticket.'
'I want to go to Bangor. What way are the trains running?'
'On the lines. There's one in ten minutes. If they're still there.'

These were the exchanges between an unexpected guest and her hostess:
'Ye'll take a drap a tay; a've just a taypot wet?'
'Naw, thank ye. I'm onny after me tay at home.'
'Ach away. Another drapa tay niver killed nobody.'
'Well, just ta plase ye. A cup in ma haun here at the fire, but mind ye a'm onny after a fry an sausages so a'm.'
'Sure a drappa tay is far sweeter, warmer and thicker than a cuppa tay any day.'
'Mebbe you're right.'

The factory's quiet wee man had notched up another small triumph, his sixth. Mother and child were doing well.
'Six. That's not a family, it's a private army,' said one of his

167

workmates.

'Before long he'll be sayin it's cheaper by the dozen.' said another.

A third remarked, 'He'll be having a quare head count every night after this.'

To him, however, it was just another day. 'Right enough,' he murmured. 'It's wonderful what ye can gather up as ye go along.'

A woman carrying a dance frock over her arm on her way from the cleaner's was stopped by a friend who said, 'That's a lovely looking dress.'

'Aye, it's my going away one.'

'Going away? Where to?'

'Nowhere.'

'That's silly.'

'No it isn't. I'm leaving it by for the time my chin's tied up.'

Two women were discussing the husband of one of them and one asked, 'What's thon I see on your man's lip?'

'Ach, he just took a notion.'

'I thought for a wee minnit his eyebrow had dropped.'

'You may well laugh. That bittava tash he's tryin to grow is an oul nuisance. I giv him a bit av my mind before we came out.'

'Yiu were just right. It's diclus.'

'I tole him there was more hair on a goosegab. Now the oul ijit's in a huff and won't come out with me.'

An assistant at the pharmacy counter in a Belfast store faced a girl of sixteen and asked, 'Can I help you?'

'Smears.'

'What do you mean?'

'Smears.'

'What is it you'd like me to give you?'

'Swacks.'

'Is it painful?'

'No. Sard.'

The message the girl wanted to convey was that she had wax in her ears.

A Co. Antrim woman was telling a neighbour of a pain in her arm and complained, 'Heaven knows what it is.'

'Does it bother you much?'

'I can't get the toothpaste outa the tube.'

'Why don't you ask your daughter about it?'

'That wouldn't do any good.'

'After all she's a hospital nurse.'

'I wud never ask her. You'd be getting your jaws tied up before she'd even notice you were dead.'

COURTS Those involved in legal proceedings inevitably reflect local attitudes. A policeman, describing a visit to the home of an offender, said he had asked, 'Have you anyone else living here with you?' and was told 'Yes, my father and mother and his oul lady and oul lad.'

A Co. Armagh woman charged with assault was said to have bitten off part of the victim's ear. She was told, 'You are fined £5 and you will be bound over to keep the peace for six months.' Immediately she protested, 'I don't mind the fine. It's keeping the piece that bothers me. I spit it out and a dog ran away with it.'

An error was made in the Christian name of a man accused of a motoring offence. He decided not to go to court but arranged for his brother to be there to see what happened. There was silence when the offender's name was called. It was called again, then a third time, when a shout came from the gallery. 'There's no such man.' The court clerk retorted 'But who are you?' Back came the reply, 'I'm his brother.'

CURES Old-time cures still have a dogged following. Many people will resort to them before deciding on a visit to the health centre—and even after a dose of aspirins and the help of valium. Folk remedies exist for nearly every complaint, with the possible exception of a heart attack or a fractured skull. Cobwebs, starch, onions, vinegar, pepper, fat bacon, the cork of a whiskey bottle and a host of other elements are the simple requirements.

If a friend of a sufferer from warts said, 'I'll give you 2p for them,' and the coin was handed over, the transaction was considered an infallible method of getting rid of them, on the grounds that they had been sold. Another cure was to rub them with soil which would then be thrown after a funeral. 'As the corpse withers so will the warts,' was the thinking.

Cobwebs wrapped round a cut finger were looked on as certain healers, while a cure for mumps was to give a ferret a saucer of milk, wait while it drank most of it, and then give what was left to the sufferer. It had to be swallowed on the spot. A handy guide to survival took the form of a verse:

To cure whooping cough I'll tell you what,
Crawl under a donkey that's wearing a hat.
For a stoonin' corn there isn't a doubt
A bit of fat bacon will soften it out.
Should a fish bone ever stick in your throat
Down a raw egg and away it will float.

A little girl suffering from head sores was required to have her hair cut very short and the scalp covered with a poultice of thick starch, the hotter the better. Not quite in this category was the boy who couldn't keep food down. A woman with the same maiden name as his father had to give the boy a slice of buttered bread and jam. 'His stomach will be as right as rain in a day or two,' was the belief.

Another child nursing a sore throat was soon back to normal after being persuaded to eat an onion saturated with pepper. While he did so it was essential that a towel soaked in cold water

169

be wrapped round his neck.

Getting rid of ringworm called for simple treatment in many homes. This consisted of dropping a penny into a jar of vinegar, leaving it until the vinegar turned green, and rubbing the affected spots with the liquid. Usually the patient was assured that they could have the penny to buy sweets.

A sufferer from cold sores around the mouth could dab the sores with a cork soaked in the dregs of a bottle of Irish whiskey.

Getting rid of chilblains was no trouble if there was a baby in the house. All that was needed to banish them was to dab them with a baby's napkin—freshly wetted by the baby.

The older generation, it is suspected, spent endless hours trying out answers for this or that cause of domestic crisis. A glass of hot milk lavishly laced with pepper eased a stomach cramp. A soft corn between the toes could be disposed of by cushioning it from its neighbour with a piece of fat bacon. The white of an egg smeared over a cut stopped bleeding. A cure for a severe cough was to scoop a hole in a turnip, fill it with brown sugar, and slowly sip the juice.

A 98-year-old Comber pensioner was well known for his brew made from beer with the juice of boiled nettles, and stirred with a red hot poker. It was his regular nightcap.

Those who suffered from stomach pains which refused to shift had only to resort to the simple expedient of placing their shoes on the fender at night, with the heels turned towards the grate.

This was rather less complicated a procedure than a reputed cure for styes. This involved a married friend of the victim's mother touching them nine times with the edge of her wedding ring, turning the ring each time. Reckoned to be equally effective where an ulcer was the complaint was to take a raw egg in which the pounded shell was stirred.

The extent to which faith plays its part in reliance on folk cures is illustrated by the claim of the elderly Londonderry man who swore that catarrh would have made his life a misery but for his daily routine for keeping it at bay. Each morning, as soon as he rose, he would take three sips of lukewarm water 'in the name of the Father, Son and Holy Ghost'. The same incantation was used in many other cases where the cure had to be drunk.

A strongly-held belief in Tyrone was attached to the marriage of two people with the same surname. They were considered to have acquired an ability to charm away all kinds of pains and aches. A Tyrone woman of ninety-six asserted that she never had a doctor in her life because every time she had a complaint she would rub the spot with whiskey, then have a small glass herself, on the premise that 'a little inside

170

and out is the best cure of all.'

It is seen that although the remedy was often as drastic as the distress it was designed to relieve, this did not dismay the patient. Still to be found are believers in a cure for a skin rash which entailed licking a frog's stomach three times and then spitting into a fire which had been burning for three hours.

There does not appear to be any record of an antidote for 'a pain in the neck'.

CUSTOMS These come and go, die away and are suddenly revived, only to fade away again. Ulster is richly endowed with them.

Many relate to a specific day of the week. It is unlucky to empty the grate, pick flowers, have your hair cut or cut it yourself on a Sunday. For some reason this does not apply to shaving.

Still remembered in many households is the old saying, 'Never cut your nails on the Sabbath morn or you'll rue the day you ever were born.'

To clean your windows on a Monday brings the risk of ill luck for the rest of the week. It is looked on as unwise to start a new job, set out on a journey or begin a task on a Friday.

Many people, when told they can leave hospital on a Saturday, will ask to be allowed to stay till Sunday. Saturday is also considered a day of ill omen on which

to move house. The basis in each case is the belief that, 'a Saturday flit means a short sit.' To bring peacock feathers or hawthorn into the house is also to ask for trouble. Misfortune is in store if you persist in stirring your tea to the right. Good fortune is sure to follow if you turn around the coins in your pocket when you see a new moon.

To have a brush thrown after you when you set out to be interviewed for a new job is considered a good omen. One woman said, 'When I left the house for an interview my husband threw a brush after me for luck and nearly broke my ankle. But I got the job.'

Another pre-interview custom is to put your left foot out first when you set off.

It is asking for trouble for two people to look into a mirror at the same time, or to take a photograph of a relative's grave.

A useful precaution during lightning is to place all the knives, spoons and forks on the kitchen floor.

The smell of roses is a certain cure for a headache and if a cat sneezes near a bride-to-be it means she will have a happy marriage.

Putting a new pair of shoes on the table can bring disaster, as can opening an umbrella indoors. To allow a red-haired person to first-foot you on New Year's morning also invites calamity.

When visiting a friend who has moved house a present of salt

171

should be brought and a few grains sprinkled in every room. This ensures 'a happy flit'.

Immediately someone dies the windows of the room in which they passed away should be opened to enable the spirit to depart.

If you own a hen which isn't laying, a certain remedy is to place some red flannel in the nest.

Still faithfully observed by many of today's bridge players is the custom of rising and walking round your chair as a remedy for bad hands. This was done in many rural areas by those who played less sophisticated domestic games like whist or ludo.

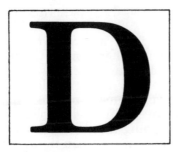

DEATH Reflecting the resigned approach to departure from this life, often encountered, is the comment of the aged Co. Antrim woman when told of the passing of yet another old friend: 'It looks as if the Almighty's forgot all about me.'

A tenant who had just moved into a small kitchen house was asked what she thought of it and replied, 'It'll do me my day. The only thing that's wrong with it is that you can't turn on the stairs. A coffin would never go up nor a corpse come down them.'

A bereaved husband, asked at the graveside how many were in the family plot, answered, 'She's the third, and if God spares me I'll be the fourth.'

On a stormy night a bus passenger commented to her companion, 'I'm thinking my ma's as well dead than running about on a night like this.'

A mourner at an Omagh funeral said of the deceased, 'She told me she was forty-nine but that must have been the number on her door.'

A Co. Down man decided to erect a monument to the memory of an uncle who had left him a generous legacy. He asked a monumental sculptor, 'How much would it take to put up a stane, say a word or two about him, and rail him in?'

Overheard at a Ballyclare funeral, 'Poor Minnie. There's one thing—the family didn't affront her. Look at them handles on the coffin. They're as long as your arm.'

The sexton in a poor parish in Co. Tyrone was consulted about the erection of a memorial on the church wall. 'It will be very welcome,' he replied. 'It will take the bare look off things. Please God we'll have room for more like it.'

When a widower returned dejectedly from his wife's funeral, his married sons and daughters tried to console him by saying he could stay with each of them in turn, and that he wouldn't be lonely. 'That's not what's worrying me,' he pointed out. 'I was just thinkin' about the oul ijit that I am, forgettin' to take aff herself's weddin' ring before she was buried when I cudda used it again.'

A minister returning from a funeral noticed a parishioner working in his garden, and said, 'I'm surprised you weren't at John's funeral.' 'Are ye?' came the reply. 'I didnae go to his funeral for he won't be going tae mine.'

A youth, sent to the undertaker's for a shroud, was questioned on the size required. 'Ah don't know the size. It isn't for masel,' he replied.

A Co. Tyrone man was told, 'That's a terrible bad cough you've picked up.' He answered, 'Ach, a don't know about that. There's people in the graveyard would be glad of it.'

A 'meals on wheels' volunteer called on a woman whose husband was awaiting burial. 'Where will I put the dinner?' she inquired. The widow pointed to the open coffin and said, 'Just put it in there, so long as you don't cover his face.'

As a funeral passed on a wet day the comment was heard, 'That's poor oul' Mary Dodds they're buryin'. Isn't the sowl gettin' a terrible day for it?'

(see WAKE)

DESPERATION Condition frequently experienced but indicated in different terms. 'I'm desperate for a drink', and 'He's desperate for a woman', imply the same degree of anxiety although they are not in the same class as 'The situation is desperate'.

A neighbour can be 'a desperate nuisance', while 'a desperate man' is usually someone who can easily get his companions into trouble during a night out, a person whose actions are unpredictable.

'A desperate speaker' describes an indifferent orator, an insufferable bore.

'Desperate weather' can embrace gales in June and snow in July, and 'a desperate job' connotes a lawn constantly in need of cutting by a reluctant gardener.

'I'm desperate' usually indicates an urgent desire to go to the toilet.

DOHERTY A name long associated in Tyrone, Armagh and Derry with a host of old-time sayings, many still to be heard. In Armagh, when the potatoes were cooking on the fire, the woman of the house would chant:

> The tatties are boilin and that's a great joke,
> For the herrins are comin in Doherty's boat.

The name figures in another common saying:

> Your grannie was a Doherty,
> True to the blood,
> And wore a tin nightcap,
> The time of the flood.

This was probably a nonsense verse used as a nursery rhyme to pacify children at bedtime.

DONKEYS Constantly used as an abbreviation for *donkey's* *years*, otherwise a long period of time.

A motorist, upset at the non-delivery of a new car, will complain to the dealer, 'I'm fed up. I've been asking you for donkeys.'

A woman in a supermarket will protest, 'I've been waiting in this queue for donkeys.'

A Housing Executive applicant will insist, 'I've been coming here for donkeys.'

A Belfastman, angry that someone he had been trying to telephone always seemed to be out, insisted, 'I've been calling for donkeys.'

A secretary, who has spent hours searching for a letter to the boss which she has mislaid, will declare, 'I'm looking for donkeys.'

DON'TS Awareness of a number of these is invaluable for the stranger. Don't, for example, inquire 'Where?' if told, 'I haven't been.' Don't be tempted to ask ironically, 'Do you plan to put them on the mantelpiece?' if told, 'I bought a pair of shoes but they aren't for wearing.' This indicates they are for special occasions. They are in a different category to the pair bought by a woman, 'Just for walking behind the child's pram.'

It is asking for trouble to inquire, 'What's his position on the team?' when informed of a footballer, 'He uses the wrong fut.' This has the same meaning as, 'He digs with the wrong fut', which should not be taken to refer to a left-footed gardener.

If it is said of someone, 'He walks', it is unwise to inquire 'What's so strange about that? I walk to the office every day myself.' In all these cases the reference is to someone of a different religious persuasion to the speaker.

When buying a loaf at 10p and the shopkeeper offers you two for 19p, causing you to comment, 'That isn't much of a reduction', don't assume he is speaking literally if he says, 'Do you want jam on it?' The message is that you are expecting too much.

DOUBLE - BARRELLED NAMES John Willie and Samuel James are common varieties of the rural Ulster custom of giving children double-barrelled Christian names intended for regular use. Rubgy international Willie John McBride is better known on the sports pages as Willie John than by his surname.

The same is the case with other bearers of this style of nomenclature, such as Samuel Joseph and William James. Their surnames are rarely used.

A wife asked by a caller seeking her husband 'Is Mr —— at home?' will often answer, 'Samuel James is down in the meadow', or, 'Samuel James is away upstairs to put his head down for a wee minute.'

Ulster kitchen comedies are full of examples of the custom. A double-barrelled name usually

175

labels a member of the cast as a well-off farmer.

In those areas where *Hugh* is pronounced *Cue* (as distinct from Belfast, where the general form is *Shue*) it does not imply that Cue John is an expert snooker player. Women are not immune from the tradition, Mary Jane being the best known form.

The christening custom is common in North America, taken there by Ulster settlers. However, in many cases only the initial of the second name is used, producing such examples as William J., Donald T., and even Harry O.

DOWN, COUNTY (population 340,009). Embraces the Ards peninsula, noted for its pawkiness.

A man paying a call on a friend was told by the man's wife, 'He's in bed with a bile. He's giving me a pain in the behine moanin' about it.' In fact he was suffering from a boil.

A guest invited to have a cup of tea is apt to reply, 'A dinny like it in a cup—it is ower wee. A dinny like it in a tin—it's ower warm. A dinny like it in a bowl—it's ower thick in the lip. A wud rather hev it in a mug.'

A visitor in Newtownards arrived while the woman of the house was baking. Her small son was playing about in the room, causing the caller to say, 'Hi boy, yer breeks is a flure behine.' The lad's trousers, in other words, were marked with flour.

A motorist on tour asked a villager for directions to a destination beyond Saintfield. He was told, 'Feth, you're a brave wee wheen of miles from where you're headin', but you push on and you'll come till a loanin' on your left haun. Take the next by-road past that and it'll bring you as far as Sanfeel, and you'll be nearer where you went to go than you are here. Does that please ye?'

A traditional South Down rhyme runs:

The sun has set or sunk
The moon has rose or risen
He slowly put his haun in her's
And she put her's in hisen.

Illustrating Co. Down's way of putting things is the small boy who dashed into a Portavogie shop exclaiming, 'The Doreen Girl's just abin the harbour. She hes her heid doon like a soo an must be haying a hundred cran.' His message was that a local fishing boat was on its way in, loaded with herring.

If it is said of someone: 'He has piles', it should not be assumed he is suffering from haemorrhoids. On the contrary he is well off, a valued friend of his bank manager.

DRINK Covers every form of liquid refreshment, whether lemonade or liquor, porter or absinthe, stout or ginger ale, claret or Coke.

'There's a drink in it for you', promises anything from a pint of Guinness to a large Scotch as a reward for doing a job or a favour.

'Do you take a drink?' seeks to find whether or not there is a danger of you being an alcoholic and thus 'drinking the bit out'.

'Had he drink on him?' aims to establish if someone was (a) palatic (b) bluthered (c) flying (d) legless (e) putrid (f) as full as the Boyne (g) nicely (h) smashed (i) poleaxed (j) on the sauce (k) plastered (l) away w' the band (m) stovin (n) scuppered.

The inquiry, 'Watter ye hevvin?' is a serious invitation to accept hospitality, as is, 'You stannin?'

EDUCATED To qualify for the compliment of being described as 'educated' calls for a wide range of attributes. You need to be 'well spoken', never talk about your bowels, go to the lavatory and not 'the classit' when the occasion demands, take one spoonful of sugar in your tea, not three or four, refer to 'rugger' not 'rugby', be able to 'fill in forms' without difficulty, and have a taste for smoked salmon when eating out.

A conversation between someone educated and someone who is not took place in a home bakery when a customer ordered, 'Six baps and six budgie rolls, and put them in separate begs.' He was asked, 'Is it the baps or the rolls in separate bags?' The reply was, 'Both.'

In the course of a discussion a visitor to the family murmured 'As Shakespeare said, "Man's inhumanity to man makes countless thousands mourn."' It brought the comment, 'Isn't it nice to have a wee bit of education.'

Of a youth whose conduct was considered exceptionally good it was said, 'He's not a bad boy at all. He's an obliging sort, and educated, too.' An immediate retort was, 'An ordinary young rascal you can keep your eye on, but the divil outa hell couldn't watch an educated one.'

Another definition of 'educated' surfaced when the statement was made, 'Tomorrow wid be the day about six weeks ago when it happened,' inspiring the comment, 'When she said that I knew she had a great head for dates. She mustav been a grate scholar.'

EXCUSES There are illustrations galore of ingenuity in providing an alibi, explaining away a chronic inability to be punctual, or excusing forgetfulness. The gift is common to young and old.

A schoolboy pleaded, 'It isn't my fault I'm late, miss. My big sister bate me to the bathroom.'

Another claimed, 'My morr cudden get the car started. She called it an oul' bitch.'

Still around are the descendants of the boy who insisted he saw a notice saying, 'Mind the steam-

178

roller,' and argued, 'I minded it till the driver came.' Today's variants of this involve heeding injunctions to 'Mind the dog' and 'Mind the tar'.

Most common alibi is 'I slep in.' Tyrone people are as prone to this as Armagh, Antrim and Down folk.

Explanations for unpaid bills are wide-ranging. A woman whose husband was receiving sickness benefit wrote, 'I can't pay you anythink this week. My husband's sick hasn't come but the minnit it comes through the letter-box I'll let you have it.'

Said of a school absentee, 'I had to keep the wee lad aff for he was bunged up with the cowl. The snatters were trippin' him. I hope he doesn't smit the rest of them for there'll be the quare pantomime.'

A despairing appeal said, 'Please excuse Joe from staying for school lunch. He's rarin' a thrush and I can't stand cuttin up the worms.'

EXILES The exile doesn't exist who fails to prick up his ears at the sound of a familiar accent far from home.

A Belfastman who had settled in Bristol and set up as a taxi driver established an instant rapport with one exile by asking her, 'Whaur till?'

An Ulster couple shopping in London were discussing whether or not to buy some knitwear and came to the conclusion, 'We could get just as good at home and a bit cheaper.' A tall young man leaned towards them said 'Carract,' and moved on. 'That's made our day,' they decided happily.

FANLIGHT Semi-circular window over the front door of older style terrace houses. Often used to give personality to the abode and for the display of such evidence of this as a stuffed bird or artificial plants. An ostentatious householder will be contemptously referred to with, 'Her and her stuffed duck in the fanlight! Make ye sick.'

In some cases stuffed rabbits have been known but there were also stuffed parrots. Fanlight taxidermy, sadly, is dying out.

FEET A subject of constant preoccupation. Footlore is almost as extensive as folklore. The woman who complained, 'I'm walked aff my feet luckin' for wide fittins to let my bunions out', is not uncommon. One announced, 'I'm quaren careful with my feet since I was sick and the doctor told me he nivver knew till he got me into bed that I had pneumonia in them.'

Comment in a shoe shop: 'I've found out why it was John Bunyan who wrote the Pilgrim's Progress. Bunions would make anybody feel they were like pilgrims.'

Heard in a bus: 'My man said his new shoes were kriplin him and his big toe was as black as the ace of spades, so I towl him to lave them aff till he gat them broke in.'

A woman in a shopping queue who admitted she had 'bad feet' was given the advice: 'Go to the charapadist. Wire yer shoes is pinchin yer feet or yir feet is pinchin yer shoes go to the charapadist. I was there last week. Ingroan toe nail, hard skin, saft corn. He tuk them all away. My feet was like new.'

A woman commented witheringly, 'My oul fella will nivver hev athlete's fut for he nivver run a yard in his life.'

A shoe shop assistant was told, 'I gat a pair of them patient shoes and they're light in the haun all right but when you have them on they're like clogs. The price isn't aff the sole yet.'

Another customer declared, 'I have a neighbour and you can see the pain of her bunions on her

FEED THE PIGS IN THEM

face. See me? Them teetering heels is right for the young ones but I'll just stick till my wearin shoes.'

A man who said he saw a Linfield forward score with three headers insisted he was that good 'he had no need of his feet'.

A shopper in Londonderry vowed that, 'Them plastic shoes fairly draw your feet so they do.'

A woman badly cut by treading a broken bottle was carried to the doctor. As she was taken into the surgery she exclaimed, 'Oh doctor. You should see the bad hand I've made of my foot.'

After an exhaustive session with a customer who tried on nearly every shoe in the shop, the assistant was heard to say, 'I can't get that woman's feet outa my head.'

The woman who said, 'I wore them shoes for a week before I put them on', was indicating that she did not go out in them for that period.

Another request was for a pair of heavy boots, 'brave and strong for I have to milk the cows in them at six and feed the pigs in them at eight.'

There was once a demand for, 'A chape pair of shoes just for him to kick about the house.'

A woman told a friend: 'Just put your feet in a bus and you'll be welcome any time.'

Anyone who 'digs with the wrong foot' has religious beliefs not shared by the speaker.

A shoe shop assistant, when advised that the shoe a customer had tried on would satisfy him, said: 'Will you go to the front and

181

see it your other foot's on the rack?'

A man coming out of a shoe shop said, 'I was trying on a pair and the girl said, 'They'd be a better fit if you took your socks off.'

FOCALS Strictly speaking these are spectacles with the lens made in two sections, but they also describe the songs provided by pop group vocalists, as in, 'Milly does some great focals', and, 'You should hear Kathy doing "When you and I were young, Maggie". She can fairly sing. The group would be a dead loss without her focals.'

FRY Generic name for a meal of fried eggs, sausages, bacon, soda and potato farls. The hotel, restaurant or boarding house where guests are given 'a fry for breakfast' is considered superior.

'He's dyin about a fry' is a man who is reckoned to know his onions.

'A fry puts you on your feet' connotes a meal guaranteed to 'warm the cockles of your heart'.

The woman of whom it is said, 'She knows how to do you a fry', can have no higher tribute paid to her.

A fry is outstanding for its flexibility. It can be served with a pot of tea for lunch, dinner or supper.

A man working in his garden who hears the call, 'Would you come in for your tea, it's a fry', is given a message which needs no translation.

Fried bread is also known as 'dip'. A Belfastwoman told a neighbour, 'When we were in Malta last year I asked the waitress could we have dip and she gave me a look. Only another woman told her what we wanted we could have been there yet.'

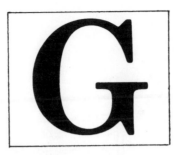

GLORY HOLE Space under the stairs in terrace-type houses. Used for the storage of household articles not necessarily discarded. A place for the child's bicycle, brushes, mops, shoes, slippers, sticks for the fire, dusters. Also used for hanging wet raincoats and setting the mousetrap. Known in some homes as the 'coal hole'. It is always unlit.

Obstreperous children would be threatened: 'If you don't be good you're for the glory hole.' It is the 'sin bin' in the households of today.

GOOD JOB When a North Antrim man says, 'It's a good job you did', he is not praising the job so much as seeking to draw attention to the serious consequences which would have followed if the action had not been taken. A young farmer who had just got engaged was met by a friend who said, 'A hear yer ganty merry Martie Magee?' 'I hope to—in the summer,' was the reply. 'Ah'll houl ye, me boy, she'll houl tae ye,' came the approving comment. It indicated that the girl would be able for her man at every turn. Years afterwards he was able to say, 'It was a good job I married Martie. We have had a grand time together and my friend was dead right.'

GREETINGS These take many forms and can often confuse the visitor. 'Har-ye?' voices friendly concern about the state of your health, as does 'You awri?' and 'Hunky dory?' 'Bite ye?' does not mean that the speaker is asking if the dog you have at your heels is liable to turn vicious. It is again showing an interest in how you are, a version of 'How about ye?'

HALF Often crops up in statements intended to be ironic. 'He wasn't half bad' means he could have been a lot worse.

'He didn't half run', conveys that he went at a right lick.

'She didn't half give it to him', denotes severe censure.

'A man and a half', 'a dog and a half', 'a horse and a half', and 'a party and a half' are all examples of the exceptional.

On the other hand, to be 'half cut' is indicative of less than normal sobriety, and 'half dead' signifies extreme inactivity.

HARDWARE Owners of shops specialising in hardware take in their stride requests that call for real resource. Many of them are far from straightforward:

'I want a dog lead for my mother.'

'Could I see your earrings? I just got my ears permed.'

'Would you have a ball for this bloody wee bitch of ours?'

HEALTH A perpetual topic among both sexes.

Asked, 'Does your stummick bother ye as much?' A sufferer replied, 'Not after I got till sixty. The stummick just left me then.'

At a health centre a woman told her friend, 'I'm still on the rhubarb and bran for I don't want to see thon dacter again if I can help it.'

Another overheard comment was, 'My man's not at all well. He's on a stick.'

One odd remark was, 'She says she's sufferin' from hallucinations but I think she's onny imaginin' it.'

A Co. Down farmer, describing an operation, summed it up in the words, 'They just took tools and wrought on me.'

A patient in a doctor's waiting room said, 'He's a great wee man. He gave my husband a cure for his piles and he hasn't looked behind him since.'

HOME BAKERY An institution in every shopping area, since bread has a role at practically all meals.

A woman returning an unsatisfactory purchase complained

185

AN ULSTERMAN WILL LAUGH HEARTILY AT HIMSELF

angrily, 'Call that a barm brack! Ye cud ride a bicycle through the curns.'

Some home bakeries will excel in wheaten bread, others in their soda farls.

A testimonial to one establishment ran, 'Not many cud houl a candle to it for the cake they soul me. Whatever they put in it—it ferly riz.'

A hostess will not hesitate to acknowledge that the cake a guest admires was not her own work. She will say quite frankly,

'Spaught', emphasising that there is nothing shameful about having bought it in a bakery.

HOUL One of the key words vital to an understanding of the complexities of the Ulster vernacular. If the reader can 'houl his hurry' he will learn that there is 'houl in', meaning restrain yourself, and 'houl out', meaning don't give in, 'houl back', implying wait, and 'houl forth', meaning talk. 'A houl you he's lying' expresses strong suspicion. There are motorists who 'houl till the crown of the road', and won't 'houl be the rules' to let a faster car pass. 'Houlin' a bus' means keeping it waiting until you're ready to go. 'Houl yer breath' is a request to stop and listen, and 'houl yer temper' is a plea not to get excited. 'Houl yer peace' and 'Houl yer tongue' are calls to take it easy, as is 'Houl on there', although this can be addressed by a horseman to his mount. An appeal not to 'houl it over me' expresses the wish that something you have done should not be cast up in a derogatory way. 'Houl yer fire' suggests that you should withhold criticism until you have heard an explanation. Anyone who agrees that all this will 'houl water' deserves praise for endurance.

HUMOUR The natives usually have a sharp sense of humour and, as a rule, can tell a story uncommonly well because of this. The Dubliner has wit, but his sense of humour has some deficiencies. He will not laugh at himself but will laugh at others. An Ulsterman will laugh heartily at himself. He will not see anything questionable if told of the customer in a Co. Down cafe who ordered, 'Two slices of toast, burnt as black as your boot, three slices of fat bacon half fried, and a cup of black coffee,' and then explained, 'A hev worms and anything is good enough for them.'

Statements will often be made to test the sharpness of the listener. This applies to a woman's comment in a fruiterer: 'See them bananas of his? If he doesn't get rid of them soon they'll be going'; and another which ran: 'Them tomatoes aren't fit for human constipation.'

To say of someone, 'They're a turn', is highly complimentary. They are the salt of the earth because they are 'good crack', are always good for a laugh, and can 'have you in fits.'

IDIOCY There are degrees of this state of mental inadequacy.

A 'buck ijit' can be defined as a literary critic who finds favour in the 'buck lep' school of Irish writing. He can also be a man who puts a lot of money on a horse which comes in last, votes for a candidate who has the lowest poll, or encourages his wife to go to a karate class.

'Buck ijits' can also be seen in television discussion panels, and on the soccer field. They can sometimes be heard reciting 'The tip of me oul cigar' at house parties. Many of them take up political careers.

INSULTS Colloquial speech is rich in insults. They embrace every known character deficiency, and cover all kinds of oddity.

A gossip is summed up in, 'She has a mouth like a pillar box— always open.'

A grumbling mother said of her son's choice of bride, 'My Johnny married a tin opener.'

A reply to the comment, 'She gave me a nasty look', can be, 'She had one before I met her.'

Other examples: 'He was that long getting his hand into his pocket I thought he was paralysed'; 'He's a slippy tit—even comes into the house like a drop of soot'; 'Mean? Him? You might as well look for the grace of God on a mushroom or wool in a goat house as expect him to pay his way'; 'He wouldn't open his mouth for fear he would waste his breath'; 'That woman has a voice that would crack a tay pot'; 'He's that near he stews his false teeth for gravy,'; 'She's that mangey she wouldn't give you two drops from her nose'; 'He wouldn't spit in your mouth if your teeth were on fire.'

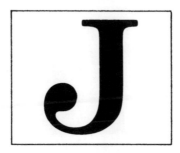

JAR A welcome drink; also a hot water bottle.

'You're always sure of a jar in Jimmy's', indicates that he is a man with 'a givvin' haun', a generous host.

An Ulsterwoman on holiday in Derby asked her English sister-in-law for a jar for her small son at bed-time. 'You start them young in Ulster, don't you?' she commented, making for the strong drink cupboard.

No alcoholic undertones are involved, however, in the suggestion, 'Leave the door on the jar.'

JOKER 'A joker and a half', or 'A bit of a joker', is someone who is perpetually striving to raise a laugh. They never tire of telling the story of the two Belfastmen sweltering in 91° on a Spanish beach on the 12th of July. One says 'I've just remembered the date. Man aren't they gettin' a great day for the Twelfth at home.' A joker will speak of an acquaintance as 'The kind of fella that would want to be put into the non-smoking part of a lifeboat', will say of the food in Majorca, 'It was all right but I got sick of the muckaroni', and is apt to make frequent allusions to: 'Big Sammy. Every time he gets back after a walk to the corner the hum of his feet is desperate.'

JUICE Before decimilisation this was the slang term for twopence, as in 'Lennus a juice'. If a car is 'heavy on the juice' its fuel consumption leaves something to be desired. 'Pickey juice' was once a slang description applied to Hebrews. Thankfully it is no longer heard.

189

L

LIGHT This has several different meanings.

A small boy with a cigarette asked a passer-by for a light and was sternly told, 'Run away home ye wee brat or I'll light ye on your behine.'

Someone who has suffered a shock will say, 'It took the light from my eyes.'

'I'm going to light out', indicates an imminent departure.

To be told at a soccer match, 'You're stannin in my light', specifically requests that you should move somewhere else or there'll be trouble.

Anyone on whom fortune

"HE CAN THROW YE AFF AFORE YER ON HIM!"

continually smiles 'always lights on his feet.'

LONDONDERRY (pop. 88,800). Second city in Northern Ireland. Sometimes known as the Maiden City. Residents who feel that gazetteers should have the city's entry cut by six letters and London scrapped, making it Derry, nevertheless usually acknowledge that there are problems in altering the title of the Londonderry Air. The girls somehow have never come to be known as Derry maids.

Sometimes known as the home of the 'surely folk', as natives seeking to indicate their agreement with a statement will say 'Aye surely'. They will do so if invited to have a drink, a cigarette, a cup of tea, or to go for a walk along the banks of the Foyle on a spring evening.

It is a city of hard-working, industrious people, the speech marked with a distinct lilt so that if a stranger asks the way the reply is said to sound so melodious that if you don't know the music you're lost.

It boasts a considerable number of *Daritys*, otherwise Dohertys.

Speaking of a pet pony a native said, 'He can throw ye aff afore yer on him. He just gives the head a jark, pulls the rains outa yer haun, and tosses ye over his head like a spinning jinny.'

Overheard at a city health centre: 'The wife can hardly spake way her beck. Now she's away to hospital way her nose.'

Of a couple going steady it will be commented: 'I saw them lunk arm in arm.' And to signal readiness for his breakfast a man will call to his wife from bed, 'Hate me trousis. A'm gettin up.'

MASTERMIND This BBC memory contest has produced many formidable Northern Ireland challengers. Its popularity has given rise to the legendary tale of a Belfast contender who set up a record in passes. It went like this:

'What is the name of a Belfast thoroughfare which starts with Donegal?'

'Pass.'

'What is needed to gain a seat in the Parliamentary Press Gallery?'

'Pass.'

'What kind of a book are you given when you open a deposit account at your bank?'

'Pass.'

'You are playing bridge and your partner bids one spade. You have no face-cards in your hand. What do you reply?'

'Pass.'

'How is a card described which allows you to travel free by train?'

'Pass.'

'You are driving along a motorway and a lorry in front of you slows down to five mph. What do you do?'

'Pass.'

'What does an Army sentry say to you if he has established your credentials?'

'Pass.'

'What word beginning with "by" describes a thoroughfare which circles round a town or village?'

'Pass.'

'What do you do with your water when you go to the toilet?'

'Pass.'

'A judge is delivering sentence. What will he do with it?'

'Pass.'

'What should a rugby player do with the ball if he wants to give it to a back?'

'Pass.'

'You are on a journey; what stage is reached which is covered by the term "pretty"?'

'Pass.'

'What is done in America if you want to get rid of a buck?'

'Pass.'

'You are a cleric seeking to indicate that an event has happened.

Where do you say it has come to?'
'Pass.'

MEDICINE In many rural districts medicine means a laxative, probably because for years this was almost the only cure given. The advent of the National Health Service has changed things, but to many of the older generation the original meaning persists.

A Ballymena doctor will understand at once when a patient asks for 'medicine for my bools'.

'He's away to the doctor for a bottle,' similarly implies the need for medicine, whether a tonic or otherwise.

This usage is not to be confused with the statement, 'My father is over eighty and doesn't use glasses. He drinks it straight from the bottle.'

OFFICE ENGLISH Examples galore of this strange vernacular can be encountered on the telephone. Answers to requests to speak to someone take many forms: 'Wud ye wait a wee tick?' 'Did youse ring?' 'Cud ye houl on?' 'He's in but he's gone.' 'Cud ye ring back after a wee while?' 'Will I tell him you called? I will if you like.' 'What are ye? I'll have to say.'

OSTENTATION Considered one of the major sins. The general feeling about it is summed up in the comment heard as a hunt was passing, the huntsmen including a local trader who was considered an upstart: 'Just luck at him. Ridin' along there as if his horse had shit marmalade.'

OVERHEARD Collectors of overheard delights have come to a paradise for the eavesdropper.

Passenger in black taxi: 'When I ast my man if his oul' pipe didden sicken him he said it would sicken him far more if he didden hev it.'

Woman at Belfast airport: 'They asked me if I would like two smokin' seats and I said I didn't mind so long as they didn't go on fire.'

Woman in supermarket: 'Lizzie's in hospital again. She'll not be at herself till she gets her legs back.'

Man in bus queue: 'The wife bought me a digital watch for Christmas. It plays "The Yellow Rose of Texas" at two o'clock in the morning. You never heard the like of it.'

Woman in bus: 'I told Mary her carpet looked lovely down and she said my shoes looked lovely on.'

Shopper in city store: 'I was talking to her next door. She has a knee.'

Customer in post office: 'The wee lad got a postcard from his aunt telling him to write soon. He sent her one back with the word "soon" on it.'

Woman shopper: 'My mother's not well at all. She's going down the drain so she is.'

194

"SHE'S GOIN' DOWN THE DRAIN, SO SHE IS"

In a public library: 'My man says a good hysterical novel is hard to beat.'

Woman in post office queue: 'Which trap should I go to? I want to know if you need a licence for a shooting stick?'

Customer in chemist's: 'The dacter said it was an infection and he gave be penniskillen for it.'

Lisburn woman to neighbour:

'In the summer if you put the butter out it runs away and if you put it in the fridge it gets as hard as a brick. A body doesn't know where to turn.'

Girl in city office: 'I asked her if she could squeeze another cup out of the teapot and she said, "Why, is it rubber?"'

Bus passenger to companion: 'The man asked me what I meant

195

when I said I wanted flires and I told him they were what you get in bookies.'

Woman in bus queue: 'The child kept us awake the whole night with abominable pains.'

Newspaper seller's advice to woman about to cross a busy street: 'Watch yerself, missus. You'd get a bumful of tin there very quick.'

Woman describing a visit to a neighbour, a chronic borrower: 'I had one look round me and, do you know, I felt more at home in that house that I do in my own.'

Ballyclare woman to friend: 'I sent the wee lad for a six-inch flower pot and he said he wasn't able to find one. The only ones in the shop had holes in them.'

Man in newsagent's: 'The wee lad kept sayin' he was freezin' an I warmed his ear.'

Woman in village shop: 'She clapsed in the kitchen and she's gettin' buried on Friday. Her other son's a plasterer.'

Laden city shopper: 'That swim-suit my daughter bought herself is only a hair's breadth from the nude. It's this television.'

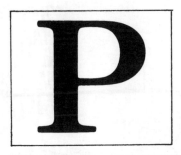

PAN One of the most used kitchen utensils; no housewife could do without one.

'I just fried the pan for our tea', denotes a meal of fried eggs, bacon, sausages and fried bread. 'I'd be up the creek without the pan', points to an exorbitant addiction.

It is an essential element in an 'Ulster fry', in equal demand after a day's work or at the end of a round of golf. The man who declares, 'I'm sick of the pan', is in a critical condition, liable to be in need of intensive care. He faces near starvation. However, the Shankill Road threat, 'I'll knock your pan in', implies the use of physical force, not an intention to cause havoc in a kitchen.

'I married a pan man', denotes (a) despair that the speaker is doomed to live with a person with a one track mind when it comes to food, or (b) the gloom of a vegetarian at the prospect of having to stare at sizzling eggs and bacon for the remainder of her days.

'I'm ready for the pan,' conveys the simple message, 'I'm starving.'

Wives will say, 'My man wouldn't go content to his work or his darts without the pan', and, 'When he comes in from the brew he's the happy man when he smells the pan.'

Families can differ in frying techniques. One will insist that the soda bread is fried and toasted in the fat, another's taste will be to 'give it a wee rummle round the pan', while some will prefer the rule, 'Don't split the farl but fry it well.' In the same category are those who say, 'Don't forget the pirta and do it on both sides.'

PETS In many cases the choice of a family pet can indicate social status. Budgies are a popular working-class choice. Attachment to them can be intense. A woman asked a shopkeeper, 'Could you give me something for our wee budgie. Its hair keeps falling out. Its driving us astray.' Another declared, 'Our budgie can't stand Channel 4. If you're watching it and the cover isn't on the cage it can change to BBC1 without you doing a thing. I wonder why it is?'

(It was established by a television engineer that the cage was close to the set, that there was a loose connection, and that when the bird flapped its wings unduly it was enough to cause the change.)

Canaries and goldfish are prized as pets in many working-class homes. One Belfastwoman told a friend, 'We just had to get rid of our three wee goldfish. My man said he was sick of them snappin' at him every night. It broke my heart so it did.'

Dogs are liked by all classes, with the larger breeds often favoured as status symbols. A woman summed up her feelings about them by saying, 'We gat a wee dog to yep at strangers. He's a great wee animal.'

The high figures at which pigeons can change hands reflect their popularity. They are often prized by those with back-yards rather than back gardens. One pigeon widow lamented, 'Know what I'm going to tell you? I sometimes

198

think I'd be far better aff in a home. All I do is keep feedin' that man of mine so he can get away to feed his oul' pigeons.'

PLACE NAMES There are many traditional rhymes associated with towns, townlands and villages. Many echo old coaching days, but are still remembered and still quoted:

Portavogie is a poor wee hole,
They burn the wrack to save the coal;
They drink salt water to save sweet milk
And they're the boys who can wear the silk.

The measurements seems to have gone wrong somewhere in:

From Augher by Clogher to Fivemiletown
Its six miles up and seven miles down
From Cullyhanna to Crossmaglen
You'll find more rogues than honest men.

There are many variations of one rhyme, depending on the origins of the person quoting it:

Lisnaskea for drinking tea,
Maguiresbridge for brandy,
Tempo is a dirty wee hole
But Rosslea is a dandy.

Another version runs:

Augher, Clogher, Fivemiletown,
Tempo is the cleanest town,
Pettigo for bottled stout
But Bangor's full of hooks and touts.

The rhymers leave few stones unturned in their efforts:

Toome for poteen,
Cookstown for stout,
Ardglass for herrings
And lie-abouts.
Ballycastle for yellow man,
Bangor for girls who want a man,
Ballyclare so sweet and fair,
Bangor for lads with Mohican hair,
Belfast for pubs that are never without,
Ballymena with nothing for nowt.

There are few places without their own special rhymes, some flattering, some denigratory:

Magheramorne for pigs and sows,
Ballygowan for brandy,
Moneyrea for baps and tay
But Cummer is the dandy.

The last line gives the dialect rendering for 'Comber'. In fact it is the Gaelic word for it.

POLAR Form of headgear; often known as a 'hard hat', more generally a bowler. A must for most funerals but now going out of fashion. Obligatory wear in a number of Orange Lodges for Twelfth of July parades. Often white gloves will also be favoured.

A woman will say, 'My man always lucks funny in his wee polar walkin' behine a hearse', but this will not induce him to discard it.

A Belfast firm kept a store of around a dozen polars in various sizes for use by executives when attending the funerals of employees. Otherwise they were never used.

199

Formerly the badge of office of shipyard foremen, gas meter inspectors and some bank messengers. In industry, 'protective headgear' has taken its place.

POLES A sport with a considerable and dedicated following. A variant of the crown poles played in England. In recent years there has been increasing support for poles under cover.

A Belfastwoman, asked if her husband was at home, explained, 'He's away out for a game of indoor poles.'

A keen polar will usually be 'known to take a drink'. Generally he is more interested in soccer than in rugby, squash or golf, and faithful about filling in pools coupons.

Considered by the retired and senior citizens to have definite advantages over more energetic sporting activities like athletics and motor-cycle racing.

POMEROY Town in Co. Tyrone liable to surprise the motorist in search of petrol. If a garage attendant asks, 'What breed does she run on?' he is trying to establish whether four star, three star or two star petrol is sought.

If the motorist stops at a pub in nearby Sixmilecross to buy a drink he may face the following inquiry when being served: 'Have ye enough thinners?' This means, 'Are you all right for mixers?'

PORN IJIT Not to be confused with pornography, merely descriptive of a person incapable of rational behaviour or thought, as in, 'The fella's a porn ijit. Says the pan for breakfast in the mornin' can damage your health'; 'Joe says the wee Glens is the goat's toe. He's a porn ijit'; 'I knew he was a porn ijit when I heard he tuk his missus to the dogs with him'; 'Alec's a porn glype. Spoke back to his morr-in-law.'

(see IJIT)

POST OFFICE A paradise for connoisseurs of overheard gems: 'I always get my stamps at the counter because they're fresher than the ones from the machine'; 'The wife said the stamp wouldn't stick to the envelope and I told her she'd licked it too much'; 'I asked for a left hand stamp and the man give me a luck. I only wanted to send the letter by air mail.'

POTATOES Prominent on every shopping list. Anyone called Murphy faces the inevitable nickname, 'Spud Murphy' spuds being known as 'murphies'.

The most commonly told potato story concerns the Ulsterman on holiday in England who complained about his boarding house dinner. When invited to explain what was wrong with it he retorted, 'Wrang with it? What was right with it? Only twa tatties, yin of them bad and the ither an onion.'

200

A lament heard in a cafe was, 'I asked for boiled potatoes and they brought me fried. Wouldn't you call that a raw deal?'

In Fermanagh can be heard the criticism, 'She's as ignorant as priddy bread at a weddin'.'

Potato farls are sometimes served with apple fillings, but these are for epicures, not gluttons. In rural areas the custom of carrying around a slice of raw potato is reckoned to ward off rheumatism. A cure for warts is to rub them with a piece of raw potato, then bury the potato.

Ways of preparing potatoes are many and varied. A tourist, describing a call at a cottage near Strangford, Co. Down, to ask for hot water to make tea, reported: 'The aged tenant asked us, "How would you like a pot of new boiled potatoes?" We jumped at the idea and watched as she filled a three-legged pot and put it on to boil. When the potatoes were almost ready she emptied out the water and covered the potatoes with several sheets of newspaper, then replaced the lit. After about five minutes the pot was removed from the fire and the potatoes turned out on to a large plate, dry and floury and bursting out of their skins. We bought a print of butter from her and we will never forget the delicious flavour of those potatoes as we sat on the sandy beach nearby and devoured them.'

PRAISE This is rarely indicated directly, but can nevertheless be sincerely meant. Examples are: 'If trouble flies in through the windy his hand is the first on the latch'; 'He's never behind the door if your cow's in the sheugh'; 'She'll always give you the len' of her smoothin' iron with a heart and a half'; 'His religion never comes aff with his Sunday suit'; 'He's never a man who would keep the top of the milk to himself.'

PRIDE Shown by many housewives in their concern about the appearance of their living conditions. Typical is the Co. Tyrone woman who got some new kitchen chairs. The children were forbidden to sit on them and had their meals standing at the table in case the chairs might be 'scuffed'.

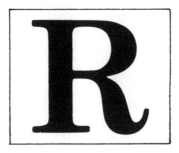

The letter 'R' is constantly ignored in everyday speech. 'On the other side of the Border' becomes, 'On the other side of the Boda.'

Commonly heard are: 'He used theatnin' language'; 'I thew it out'; 'My stummick thinks my thote's cut'; 'He doesn't thill me any more'; 'I feel as if I'm goin to tho aff.'

The usage sometimes figures in advice tendered to a boxer taking a hammering, as in, 'Tho inna tile.'

References to the 'Ministay of Health' will be heard, as well as to the Guvament'.

ROMANCE Dashing Lotharios will not be encountered at every street corner or crossroads. They are more liable to surface in a lounge bar than in an ordinary pub.

Behaviour in affairs of the heart is generally governed by a mixture of caution, prudence and circumspection rather than impetuousness and brinkmanship.

One suitor was spending a weekend at his loved one's home in the country to meet her parents. At bedtime she told him, 'We don't get up early on Sunday so just lie on till you hear me scraping the toast.' She could never understand why he lost interest from that moment.

A country girl out driving with her sweetheart on an icy, wintry evening complained: 'Just look at my hands. They're blue with the cold.' 'Why can't you sit on them, then?' he replied.

A couple out for a walk had come to recognise that their affections were cooling. An attractive girl passed and the man said, 'Did you see that? She smiled at me.' 'That's nothing,' came the reply. 'The first time I saw you I laughed out loud.'

Evidence that not all men are 'cold fish', or dour wooers, is provided by the Armagh man, rejected after years of courtship, who said, 'I headed there and then for the lough. I sat on the bank in the light of the moon, took off my shoes and socks, and washed my

"LET'S GO INTO THE SIN ROOM"

hands and feet clean of her, so I did.'

ROOM Describes a wide variety of domestic accommodation, especially rural. 'A sin room' is not one used for immoral purposes. It is simply the sitting room, often designated 'the lounge'.

In working-class homes 'the room' is also called the 'parlour'.

'The room's done' indicates that the bed has been made in the room reserved for anyone who might stay overnight.

'There's no room in the house' need not denote anything more than that the rooms are fairly small.

In country areas 'the room' is the show room of the house, reserved strictly for clerical visitations or other important occasions, often for writing a letter. It is usually kept locked, with no admission for children.

There could be no higher tribute than, 'You should see the room in her house. You could ate your dinner off the floor.'

203

SCALLIONS When abroad, Ulster people run into problems when they ask for scallions at a greengrocer's. These, of course, are known elsewhere as spring onions. In fact the Hebrew equivalent of the term is 'onions of Askelon'. 'Scallions' is clearly a corruption of 'Askelon'.

SCHOOL An important element in the background of the average native. If it is established that he is a *'Stonian* it means he has been educated at the Royal Belfast Academical Institution, often referred to as *Inns. Stonians* consider themselves superior to those educated at *Mehadie*, or Methodist College, frequently spoken of as *Clejins*, or *Cambill*, which means Campbell College.

It is safe to assume that all play rugby, cricket, squash, monopoly, golf and bridge, abhor 'Top of the Paps' and travelling in buses, and are liable to call their wives 'honey-bunch', although 'she' is sometimes used.

SHOPPING An activity which can have unusual motives. A woman will buy a new coat 'just to have it'. A Belfast trader was asked for 'a pair of men's trunks with legs in them.' Cakes will be bought 'in case somebody comes', i.e. so that they can be produced as evidence of the lavish life-style of the householder. A motorist in search of a map was shown several varieties of floor mops.

A village grocer who was asked for 'a pound of hard apples for Sybil' knew immediately what was meant. Sybil was the name of the shopper's goat. The animal would not stand still while being milked unless it had an apple to munch. One hard apple was sufficient for a quart of milk.

A Belfast shopper seeking enough wool to knit a winter coat for her pet dog was told that a better idea of the amount of wool required might be obtained if the dog were brought along. 'But I couldn't do that,' came the protest. 'I want it to be a surprise for the wee pet.'

A country draper was confronted by a customer who wanted 'a blue nightdress with long sleeves, for I throw my arms out of the bed at night and they get cold.'

A shopkeeper was asked, 'Is them eggs fresh?' and replied, 'I ain't saying they ain't.' Retorted the shopper, 'I ain't asking you is they ain't. I'm asking you is they is, is they?'

An Ulsterwoman on holiday in Scotland admired a set of antlers in an antique shop and asked the price. '£25,' she was told. 'They're offa dear,' she commented. 'Of course they're off a deer,' she was told. 'Did you think they were off a greyhound?'

It is part of the shopkeeper's life to be confronted with strange requests, such as, 'I want a pair of scissors that would cut my toes,' and 'Have you a pilla for a dive-in bed?'

Ordering carrots, a shopper said, 'I want the ones in Titchy Beggs.' The baffled shopkeeper explained that he knew of no one of that name who owned a shop. 'But you know what I mean,' persisted the shopper, 'Wee Titchy Beggs.' Finally all was made clear. What was wanted were pre-packed carrots in tissue bags.

SODA BREAD Soda bread is not now baked at home as often as formerly. Before the home-made variety has entirely vanished, here is the recipe:

Take 2lbs flour, 1 teaspoon bi-carbonate of soda, 1 heaped teaspoon salt, 1½ozs butter or margarine, 1 pint buttermilk. Sift together the flour, salt and bicarbonate of soda into a large mixing bowl. Rub in the butter and mix with the buttermilk into a good soft dough. Transfer to a floured board and flatten out to about two inches thick, shape round, then cut into four quarters or farls. These are put onto a hot, un-greased griddle and cooked on a low, steady heat for 12 to 15 minutes on each side.

SPEECH The diversity and capriciousness of the vernacular fills the air with rich, colourful language. A visitor, admiring a National Trust garden, was told, 'You want to be here in the summer when the beds is black with yellow roses.'

A woman rushed into a village grocery and called out, 'Givvus a tin of calves' milk in a hurry for the bus. I'm takin' the chile till the clink.'

Agreement with a statement will come in the form of, 'It is that', but 'I hear ye' signifies a high degree of doubt over what has been heard.

A mother will complain: 'They giv the childern burney sweets. It didden do their wee gubs any good.'

A comment will run: 'She has awful nice dark hair. Pity she made such a haun of herself.'

A farm visitor heard the loud cackling of a hen and asked, 'Is that hen lyin'?' He was instructed: 'Go on out an luck for yerself. Ye'll soon know if she has laid or lied.'

The statement, 'They are no leavin' there any more', infers that the people in question have moved house.

'Me and her's very big,' signifies close friendship.

'I wed the lawn' or 'I wed the beds' is not an indication that something has been weighed.

A passer-by, criticising the animals illustrated on the ceramic wall tiles at a butcher's, said, 'Them sheeps is awful bad drew.'

'I dropped her a hint but she never lifted it', is synonymous with the lady's inability to get the message.

A child will be warned: 'Don't speak to strangers unless you know them.'

'It's more ornamental than useful, like the curl on a pig's tail,' signifies disapproval.

'I wouldn't put it past him,' adds up to a verdict that the person alluded to is not to be trusted.

A new postman delivering a badly addressed letter was told it should be left at 'the house with the fir trees at the bottom of the road.' Later he complained to his informant: 'I had to give up. I could only see a house with two trees. There was none with four.' 'I know,' came the reply. 'I said the house with the two fir trees.'

An 80-year-old confessed: 'At my time of life you get a lot of them wee bothers that crop up. If you're no drippin' at the snoot you've twitches roun' the sholters an aboot the legs.' His listener, an Englishman, asked what was meant by snoot and was told, 'Ach ye hev yin yersel, man, right in the middle of your face, an' mine you it's a right wheeker.'

An elderly lady on the beach at Scarborough asked an Ulster visitor the time and was told, 'Ten past eight.' 'What's eight?' she wanted to know. The Ulsterman showed her his watch. 'I see what you mean,' said the woman, 'Ten past ite.'

A farmer's wife was about to have a baby and at around two o'clock in the morning her husband hurriedly set off to fetch the midwife. He knocked urgently at her window and when she called, 'Who's there?' he explained his mission. She said, 'All right. I'll be down in a minute.' He replied, 'Well, don't be long for I have my hat in my haun.'

The owner of a seaside guest house was telephoned with a request for a bedroom with a bath and toilet. 'I'm sorry,' he replied, 'I don't have one with a toilet, but I could let you have a room that overlooks the sea.'

A joiner, admiring a tight mortis and tenor joint, said, 'It's as tight as a fish's arse and it's watertight.' Discussing different hardwoods such as teak or ebony, he said, 'It's as hard as a hoor's heart.' Assessing different types of glue with a colleague, he said of

206

a new variety, 'It sticks like shit tae a blanket.'

SPORT The popularity of sports in Ulster is reflected by the fact that, whatever the game, it is capable of exciting comment at its most mordant from those following it. No fans are more explicit. Nor, indeed, more artless. Typifying the quality of some of the criticisms is this conversation between two spectators after their team had been overwhelmed:

'Our left-half left the other half at home.'

'And the centre-half only got one kick at the ball and it was a header.'

'Aye, and missed it. Our goalie would have been better with a corner flag stuck in the middle of the goal.'

'He's getting a transfer to Notts Forest. He should do well sawing down the trees.'

'Going to see the team again next week?'

'Wouldn't miss it. Sure they're not a bad wee side.'

A selection of the sayings of sports fans comes from Malcolm Brodie, much-travelled sports editor of the *Belfast Telegraph*:

At the time the death of Gigli, the Italian tenor, was being announced, Northern Ireland and Italy were playing at Windsor Park. It was a fiercely fought match and feelings were running high, when an Italian player was ordered off for a tackle on an Irish

back. As the offender was leaving the field a Belfast voice roared out, 'Put him in a box along with Gigli.'

Seeking to goad an opponent in a pub argument, a soccer fan exclaimed, 'Anyway, we've no Fenians on our team.' Quietly came the reply, 'Lucky Fenians.'

After a rough Linfield game with a Turkish team a home supporter was heard inquiring 'Them Turks—are they Prod Muslims or Catholic Muslims?'

An Irish supporter at the 1982 World Cup in Spain who was ordering two bottles of 'San Miguel' beer, addressed the waiter, '*Señor*, sir, two "Sammy Magills", *monsieur.*'

When German journalists were being given an outline of the Irish team's tactical plan they were told, 'Our whole idea is to equalise before the other team scores.'

During an Irish Football Association Council discussion one of the speakers, a constant interruptor, was told from the chair, 'Sit down or I'll have to bring my gravel down on you.'

Boxing produces barracking no less caustic than soccer. At an Ulster Hall tournament a spectator, whose view of the ring was being constantly upset by photographers' flash-bulbs, called out indignantly, 'Throw them bloody welders outa here.'

Requests to 'Start the dance music' or 'Put the lights on—I'm reading' during contests marked by lack of excitement are inevitable.

On the day when Prince Charles was being invested as Prince of Wales, Ireland beat Wales by over sixty shots in a bowls international at Mortlake. A youth studying the scoreboard was heard to murmur, 'Not much of a start for Charlie on his first day.'

An Irish supporter at another bowls international in England telephoned from his room in desperation to complain to the hotel receptionist: 'I can't find the zip in my sleeping bag.' It was pointed out that the 'sleeping bag' was, in fact, a duvet.

When snooker star Ray Reardon was told of the banning of Belfastman Alex Higgins for licking the ball before the start of a frame, he was heard to ask, 'Who would touch anything Alex licked?'

Another Ulster snooker star, Denis Taylor, after appearing in specially designed glasses, explained: 'Now I can see the pots I miss.'

A Belfastman, travelling home after a Dundalk race meeting at which he lost practically all his money, was passing the city cemetery, where one of his closest friends had been buried only a few days before. He was unable to resist calling out, 'Don't worry, Hughie. You're missin' nathin' here.'

STAR CRAVEN MAD A phrase often applied to soccer referees considered to be ineffectual. It im-

plies that he is stark raving mad and should be returned to the mental institution from which he had been let out.

A person can be *star craven mad* who expects a dry and sunny 'Twelfth', or announces he has agreed to his wife attending further education classes in Urdu, decides to buy 'a wee dug for company', or announces that he intends to 'take up palitics to pass the time.'

STARING A well-established custom, commonly described as *stern*. If you are a confirmed starer and are sitting in a crowded bus, your day is made. Your victims have no escape. Your subjects can include people wearing odd socks, someone pregnant, with a squint or ill-fitting teeth, a woman in a mink jacket, a woman wearing curlers, or anyone overdressed.

The starer can silently but effectively indicate distaste, resentment, contempt, amusement, or pity. The greater the discomfort shown by the victim, the greater the enjoyment of the starer.

If you are 'a staree' you go through agonies of remorse that you didn't wear a better suit, polish your shoes, get your hair done, spend more time with your make-up or change your socks.

Starers are responsible for governing many aspects of behaviour and dress. It is common to reason, 'If I wear an outfit like that people will stare.'

There are grounds for the argument that staring should be made an offence against the law. The challenge, 'Who do you think you're staring at?' has started many a fight. This can happen when one starer is confronted by another.

Staring is a practice at which children are particularly skilled One small boy, warned that picking his nose would give him an enormous stomach, was fascin- ated by a woman in an advanced state of pregnancy sitting near him in a bus. Finally he exclaimed, 'Hi, missus, I know what you've been at.'

A woman hobbled into a Don- aghadee surgery with her knee bandaged, a black eye, and several cuts and bruises. When asked, 'What would seem to be the trouble?' she replied, 'People keep staring at me, doctor.'

TEA Part and parcel of Ulster life. With some reason it could be said, 'The place is coming down with vivid tea drinkers.' Lack of awareness of this can confuse visitors, hence the case of the Englishwoman who was asked, 'Would you like a mouthful in your hand?' and replied, 'I wouldn't mind only I have my gloves on.' The hostess looked at her as if she had taken leave of her senses.

In many cases, 'a good cup of tea' is assessed as one on which 'a 10p piece would float.'

Tea buffs have been known to make such requests as, 'Cud ye squeeze anor cup outa the teapot?' and to make statements like, 'I threw the teapot out and forgot it had a coupla cups in it.'

It is not considered unusual for a mother to call to her child playing in the street, 'Come in fer yer tea. Spored.'

'The tea's drew', infers that a meal is ready, 'a drappa scald' is synonymous with 'a cup for drinking'.

Two extremes in tea-making are covered by the statements, 'I like tea you could trot a mouse across' and, 'It was that wake you could read the paper through it.'

Voicing appreciation of a well-brewed cup, a woman said, 'I needed that to rinse the wine away.' (It acted as a remedy for her flatulence.)

A woman complained to a neighbour, 'There I was, just settlin' down for a crack and a cuppa tea in wee Mrs Cairns's when I happened to remark as she was pouring it out, "It looks like rain." Talk about the look she gave me, but mind you the second cup was an awful lot stronger.'

A visitor was told apologetically, 'I was just going to make you a wee cup but the teapot run out on me.'

The statement, 'the tea's not right drew', affirms that it needs a few minutes before being poured.

TEETH Frequent topic of comment, especially when dentures are worn. A woman said, 'My man has more teeth in his head than the mouth of a flour bag.' This was a mere statement of fact, a

recognition that here was something he had to learn to live without.

A wedding guest said after the reception: 'I did so not enjoy it, for I never minded my teeth till we set down.'

When a house guest was asked if she had slept well in spite of the crying of another guest's baby in the next room, she relied, 'Sure when I take my teeth out I can't hear a thing.'

Despair was voiced by a Tyrone woman who insisted, 'My man's an awful nuisance in bed at night.

211

He's for ever wantin' me to reach him his teeth to bite my ears, the oul' ijit.'

THREATS Stern warnings to ill-behaved children formerly took a much more bloodthirsty form than those of today, which usually run to, 'I'll send you to your bed if you don't stop being a nuisance.'

Threats that can still be remembered by older generations were often a variant of, 'If you come home with a broken leg I'll wring your wee neck.' These were rarely taken seriously, nor was it intended that they should.

Hardly in this category, however, were warnings like, 'If you don't do what you're told I'll whitewash the kitchen with your blood'; 'Take anything more that doesn't belong to you and it won't be the police I'll send for, it'll be an ambulance'; 'I'll give you such an uppercut that you won't come down for a week if you don't stop aggravating me'; 'If you go on acting the lig I'll bate you round the balls of the leg with a teaspoon.'

One Co. Antrim admonition was: 'You keep away from that well. You could be drowned in it and anyway it's full of wee popes.'

A Belfast mother's reprimand was: 'If you don't stop botherin' me I'll pull your ears off and fry them in the pan for your dinner.'

TOILET Never in any circumstances referred to as the 'comfort station', but will sometimes be designated as 'the bog'.

There are instances where 'the toilet' is understood without actually being named. A man shopping with his little daughter in a city store felt her tugging at his sleeve and heard her whisper urgently, 'I have to go, daddy.' A woman assistant standing nearby sized up the situation and said to the man's relief, 'I'll take her along.' When they returned father beamed his appreciation and said to the little girl, 'I hope you thanked the lady.' Eagerly the youngster answered, 'Why, daddy, she had to go too.'

TRAFFIC Crossing signals have brought their own problems to those pedestrians who tend to be bewildered by heavy traffic.

A Ballyclare woman illustrated this confusion by rushing up to a group waiting for the lights to change at a busy Bangor crossing. 'Are you people waiting for a funeral?' she wanted to know. 'We're waiting for the red man,' she was told. 'What, a red Indian?' she gasped. 'We're waiting for him to turn green,' came the information. 'I never heard the like,' she objected. 'I'm going to go across anyway.' 'If you do that you'll go to a funeral all right,' she was warned, 'only you won't smell the flowers.' 'Where will I be going, then?' she asked. 'That depends on how you have lived.' 'Well, where is this red man?' she demanded. 'I cannae see one.' At that moment the crowd moved

212

forward. 'Sure I see what you mean,' she exclaimed. 'Why didn't you tell me the first time?'

Similar confusion led a Belfast woman to comment about a friend: 'She stood waiting to cross for hours for she's colour blind and between green men and red ones and them yella lines it's a miracle she ever gets anywhere, the sowl.'

TURN Can describe changing one's religion, a music hall item, or going round a corner.

'He turned' means that the person concerned has decided to subscribe to a different faith, and implies that he is not to be trusted.

A girl receiving a proposal of marriage who asks the proposer, 'Wud ye turn?', is trying to establish if he will adopt her religious beliefs and abandon his own.

The lover who agrees 'to turn' proves his sincerity as effectively as if he signs a declaration in blood.

'A quare turn' indicates a person who can be the life and soul of a party, while 'a bit of a turn' can also signify a sudden bout of illness.

TYRONE, COUNTY (population 139,037). The people are usually hospitable but tend to be rather suspicious of city folk. Their open-handed nature is echoed by the words:

Sit up to the hate, me darlin' Kate
An make yerself at home.

It reflects the same degree of warmth as the welcome, 'Come in, Dungannon, I know your knock.' The speech here is generally rich and lively.

Tyrone claims the old man who said, 'It was that coul', a hadda strip the back o' the dure.' (That is, he had to remove the coats hanging on the door and put them on the bed to warm him at night.)

213

ULSTERMAN The working-class Ulsterman has a wry sense of humour, often razor sharp. He can show truculence if he feels the occasion demands it but is basically reticent, and tends to convey diffidence about his image.

He will admit he 'doesn't know his Bible' as well as his father did, and has an ability to say of someone, 'He's a bitter wee Prod' in a tone of despair. He has an enthusiasm for bowling and/or Gaelic, depending on the district in which he lives.

He can throw a useful dart and is a different person after two or three pints. He often has a close friend called Jimmy, Alec or Malky whom he will constantly quote, particularly if they are fans of the same soccer/Gaelic player.

If he lived in England he would vote Labour yet consider Arthur Scargill 'a head case'.

If he labels someone 'a dirty yella rat', he will show a readiness to 'kick the fella's slats in'.

Depending on the school he went to, he will think with longing of the days when 'the Yard' was a hive of industry, or voice delight that those days have gone.

He will tell you, 'I went to the hairdresser's and got a clatter weak daff' and watch to see if you smile. (He is describing a severe hair cut.)

Whatever his form of worship, he is devoted to 'the pan', and will sing 'The Sash', 'Kevin Barry' or 'Danny Boy' with the least encouragement, his choice governed by where he worships.

If his wife is pregnant he will say, 'She's thon way' not, 'She's up the spout'. He will refer to her as 'the wife' or 'the missus', rarely 'my wife'.

Only infrequently would it occur to him to buy her flowers and he usually considers it improper to push the pram or the buggy when out for a walk.

He is not unduly bothered if his wife appears at breakfast loaded down with curlers, but feels uncomfortable if she has a good job.

She, too, has a lively sense of humour and would appreciate the story of the neighbour who was admiring a friend's eighteen-month-old baby. The question was asked, 'What do you call him?' The mother answered, 'Nathan', which brought the surprised comment: 'But, my Gawd, at that age surely ye must give the wee lad a name.'

She is often a frenzied knitter and will boast quietly of the things she can 'knit out of my head'.

She will display a neat sense of detail when telling a story. For example: 'A woman I know bought a takeaway and when she got it home she found a clack in it; when she looked there wasn't a leg missin'.' This affirms a close knowledge of natural history, and admiration that the lady concerned should be aware of the exact number of legs possessed by a cockroach.

UPBRINGING Family discipline varies extensively, ranging from the severe to the benign. A lot will depend on how the parents themselves were brought up. Typical of the authoritarian is the mother who was told that her small boy had fallen in the street and was 'roaring his head off'. Her reply was, 'Let him cry away there. The more he cries the less he'll pee.'

In the same bracket was the mother who had taken her young son to school for the first time. On arrival he refused to go any further and started weeping. Angrily she told him, 'Am I to leave you with a kiss or a sore behine.'

This contrasts with the father who said of his son's misbehaviour, 'Let the wee lad be. Sure I was young myself once.'

Youngsters who have been 'well brought up' are generally disliked by their peers, and are often labelled 'cissies'.

WAKE Occasion for a night-long assessment of the deceased's life, for gloom as well as joy, but now less religiously observed by city folk than in rural districts. Usually marked in the latter by a generous supply of drink. Custom insists it is unlucky to turn anyone away from a wake, whether or not they are 'friends of the corpse'. This results in considerable abuse of hospitality. The attendance can thus include, 'the corpse's cistern-law, the corpse's bror-in-law, the corpse's cousin, two of the corpse's far-out cousins, frens of the corpse but no relations, and fellas there for the drink.'

When a widow was asked for one of her late husband's shirts to make a shroud she said, 'Divil the white shirt had he', and produced a white underslip, well starched, with lace trimming on the neck and hem. 'Try that on him,' she said. 'It will do him fine well. It's myself that knows it. Every time I wore it a bline man could see the love light in his een.'

Another widow who was asked why she delayed calling the doctor explained, 'Roun' here we cure the sick werselves.' When questioned how this was done she said, 'We make the best poteen and give the sick a glass. If that doesn't work we give him another. If he still isn't better we give him another. If even that's no manner of use, well, they're not worth curin'.'

Of a man survived by four sons it was aid, 'Sure there isn't wan of them boys with the head to fill his shoes.'

Said a mourner of her deceased neighbour, 'He's the nicest corpse I've ever set eyes on. He was over six fut tall an a quare nice wee man.'

A new arrival at a wake was told by the relict, 'I asked the doctor what did he die of and he said it was mainly senility. I told him if the sowl hadn't been so stubborn he wouldn't have had it if he'd let me get the doctor sooner. He wasn't able to get it intil his saucepan head that a man has to go sometime.'

Of a confirmed agnostic who had 'passed on', a mourner said, 'He's brave and well-dressed to be goin' nowhere.'

Another widow expressed her feelings thus: 'Sure it wouldn't have been so bad if he'd waited till the weather turned a bit warmer. He won't feel the cold where he's going, but I'll have to go to the expense of buying myself an electric blanket.'

One mourner concluded his appraisal by saying, 'It was awful sudden, right enough. Many a good handshake he had in his time because of his decency. Now he's finished up with the last yin, a clap on the face with a spade.'

A surprise inquiry by one mourner was, 'Are they hevvin' a post mortal?'

The qualities of one departed friend inspired the tribute, 'There was no harm in the man at all. He had a heart of corn and that's no chaff.'

Still observed at many wakes is the custom of touching the corpse. This is said to prevent you from

217

dreaming of the deceased.

WEATHER A perpetual subject of discussion. It can be, 'a gran day for the ducks', 'a watry mornin', a day calling for the comment 'scummin' down', or 'a snifter of a night'.

The statement, 'the wire's tarble' signifies weather at its worst, while 'cat wire' is another way of saying that it is catastrophic. *Mizzlin* and *drizzlin* are less desirable conditions than *clearn* or *fairn*.

On a bitterly cold day, marked with frequent showers of hail, a housewife hurried to the door to offer shelter to the breadman. The house overlooked a rugby field where a match was in progress. The breadman commented, 'Begod if those boys were working they'd be stannin' shelterin'.'

On a torrid July day a passer-by remarked to a workman slogging away on a Co. Antrim road scheme: 'Hat, issent it?' 'Aye,' he replied. 'The clegs is the buggers a day like that, missus.'

A neighbourly inquiry on a wintry morning, 'How's your man? What about his chest?' brought the reply, 'Augh, this weather'll be the death of him. Ye should hear him haughal in the morning. You'd think it was claps of thunder.'

A Ballyclare man confided to a friend: 'It was that wet a night d'ye know the wife came home w' her backside ringin'.'

WEE SHAP A popular institution, particularly when situated on a corner. There are streets where the *wee shap* has defied the onslaught of the supermarket, largely by keeping open when the supermarket is shut. A wee shap sells nearly everything, from laces to 'brown blacknin', from 'Ferry Lickwood' to candy apples.

There are, of course, limitations, as in the case of the woman who had bought some cocktail sausages and asked the shopkeeper if he had any sticks. 'Sarry, missus,' he replied, 'we've nathin' but firelighters.'

A wee *shap* is unflustered by such requests as, 'Wud ye change that 10p into brown money'; 'Have ye a map head as the hairs are cummin' outa my oul one?' or, 'Hev ye any of that new green smellin' perfume?'

Wee shaps are a sounding board for all kinds of revelations: 'I hate them tea begs. They're useless if ye want to read your cup'; 'I don't know what to make for the dinner. I've turned agin' the pan. Mebbe I'll make a drappa tay in my haun. It might taste my mouth.'

Nine times out of ten *wee shap* proprietors tended to specialise in sweets. These provided all sorts, in every sense.

A woman's recollections of one ran: 'There was no smart window dressing. Indeed the window was always stacked with colourful empty tins. In the *shap* were such delights as 'chew chew', toffee of a delicate rose pink and exquisite flavour, egg and milk 'chew chew', nutty 'chew chew'. The egg and milk flavour was the most popular. With what anticipation we would watch the shopkeeper use his little toffee hammer to measure out our order. Chewing the egg and milk, your mouth would be filled with a creamy, delicious emulsion, sheer bliss to swallow. Swinging on a lamp-post with a mouth full of egg and milk 'chew chew' was heaven itself, and Wagga Wagg's *shap* the gate thereof.'

Memories of a wee Fermanagh *shap* were: 'It could have been there since the first Plantationists made it their rallying point for their few needs. I see yet the yellow tallow candles, ancient wooden bowls, large earthen mugs, stone storage jars, and Mary, the shopkeeper, telling me after fulfilling my order to, 'Watch the step now, daughter', as I would weave my way past bags of corn, bundles of ropes, and salty hard sides of bacon.'

Another recollection was of Candy Mary's, in Belfast's Old Lodge Road. She specialised in home-made slab toffee in six or seven varieties, including peppermint and coconut. Scales were rarely used. Once she was told, 'Please don't give me too much as I'm going back to school.'

In *wee shaps* jam would be sold loose, spooned from an enormous stone jar, also black and white linen thread which hung in hanks and sold in pennyworths.

Mouth-watering merchandise in today's *wee shaps* is different but no less varied. Their candy apples can be highly recommended, as can their toffee, yellow man and other confections—all fighting a losing battle against 'Mars Bars', 'Opal Fruits' and their attractively packaged ilk.

Above all, the *wee shap* is unbeatable when it comes to picking up gossip.

WINDOW SILL Often referred to as 'windy stool', but no longer what it was. Formerly used for the popular children's game of 'dropsies', played with cigarette cards. The object was to touch as many cards as possible with the one you dropped. You collected all those touched.

Often provided a seat for neighbours out for a gossip.

A Twelfth of July tradition is to paint the window sill red, white and blue.

'A day for the windy stool' is one that is warm and sunny.

'A fella fell aff a windy stool' is as commonly used an example of dialect speech as 'a fella fellaff a larry'.

WEDDINGS One unwritten rule about an Ulster wedding is that guests do not go to the nuptials 'on their feet'. Those who walk to the church are considered to lower the tone of the proceedings.

At a Belfast wedding one of the guests made the comment,

'Doesn't the bride look gorgeous?' which brought the reply, 'If you don't look like the Rose of Tralee on your wedding day you have slept in for you won't be worth looking at when you're sitting on the toilet years later with your jaws surrounded with flannel.'

A wedding guest, asked by an usher, 'Who's side are you on?' is not being invited to indicate where his sympathies lie, merely whether he is sitting on the bride's or the bridegroom's side of the church.

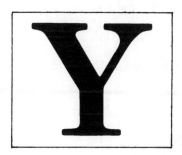

YARD This is Harland and Wolff's famous shipyard, not to be confused with an outside toilet. In its heyday it was a rich source of humour, its output of stories as colourful as its output of great ships.

It was no less rich in characters—men like 'Alec No More', so called because on the day after his promotion to foreman and the accolade of 'a hard hat', a colleague greeted him, 'Hello there, Alec.' 'Luck here,' he replied. 'It's mister from now on. I'm Alec no more.'

A newly-appointed painter was asked on his arrival at work if he had brought his cards. 'I haven't,' he answered, 'but if you like I'll bring a set of draughtsmen and a boord in the morning.'

After nearly forty years service a worker was called aside by his foreman and told, 'I'm very sorry, Bill, you and I will have to part.' 'But where are you going?' he asked 'It isn't me,' the foreman explained, 'it's you, Bill.' It then dawned on him what was happening. 'If I only had known it was a spell job,' he said, 'I'd nivver have taken it.'

A new foreman, named John Duken, had checked up on his squad, and soon after bumped into a workman a short distance away. 'I'm Duken, the new foreman,' he told the man. 'Just you stick along with me, mate,' the worker said, 'I'm juking him too.'

A shipyardman came upon a friend who was prodding at a deep pool of oily water with a long stick. 'It's my jacket,' he explained. 'It fell in.' 'Man dear, sure it wudden' be worth wearin' if ye ivver got it out,' his friend said. 'Ach, I know,' came the answer, 'but my piece is in the pocket.'

One of the characters still remembered is Big John, a riveter with a prodigious appetite. It was said of him: 'That fella has a stummick like the howl of a boat.'

There are many stories surrounding the ill-fated Belfast-built *Titanic*. Some time after the disaster a riveter is said to have been heard lamenting, 'I knew something would happen to her. A week after she sailed I found twelve rivets in my dungarees I

221

THE ACCOLADE OF A HARD HAT

clean forgot to put intil her.'

A new employee, told to find the measurements of a steel plate and not accustomed to the use of a rule, came back with the news, 'It's the size of your rule and two thumbs over, with this piece of brick and this bit of a tile, the breadth of my haun and my arm from here to there barn a finger.'

A worker, on being lifted clear after the collapse of a staging, moaned, 'I'm hurt bad. It lucks as if my futball days is over.' 'Ach away, man,' he was told. 'Sure you can still blow a whistle.'

A poor timekeeper was advised to buy a good alarm clock. 'I've got one,' he insisted, 'but it goes aff half an hour before I get up.'

A catchword that lasted for many years was inspired by a foreman who caught a worker boiling his tea-can before the lunch-time horn. The man bolted, leaving the can steaming away. Indignantly, the foreman roared after him: 'I'll boil yer can for ye.'

222

John Pepper's

Ulster
Haunbook

Illustrated by
Rowel Friers

Joey's Bowler

'Nice one,' Joey said.

'I like it,' George answered. 'Thought it was just the job. Picked it up only last week.'

'Just the job alright.' There was a faint note of patriotism in the tone.

The two men, bowler-hatted, were on their way to the funeral of Harry Carter. There was promise of a good crowd. One that would have pleased Harry, who was a man for whom everybody had a good word. He was into everything, never missed a funeral. Besides the usual important organisations, Harry was a leading light in such bodies as The Safer Streets Association, Cut Down on Supermarkets, and The Control of Bad Building Organisation. A lot of them were societies which usually lasted a month or two before disintegrating.

'Cost you?' Joey asked quietly. He had an abiding interest in bowlers. The one he now displayed with pride was kept in a Bell's dozen-whisky box on top of the wardrobe in the back bedroom. The box had been borrowed from his off licence. Every week the hat was brought out and tenderly brushed, handled as if it were breakable.

Fifteen years ago Joey had bought the hat for £5. He considered this a small fortune at the time, but it was a good make. It was after he had seen a BBC interview with a leading Orangeman who was explaining the details of his

regalia and emphasising his pride in his bowler. It was emphasised that the hat had cost £30 and that the price in London ranged up to £100.

Joey was convinced there was money in his bowler. It would be a shrewd investment. Besides, there was now the fact that he had kept a careful record of its history. It had appeared at ten Twelfth parades, at least twenty-five processions, nineteen funerals and nearly nine weddings. Its size, too, was an advantage; 7½ wasn't far from average and was easily adjustable.

'Your missus was telling the wife the interest you take in that bowler is powerful,' George was saying. 'Wife was talking to her last week. Ye know women.'

Joey gave him a sideways look. At home his interest in the bowler was a sore point. The last time it had been an issue he had been accused by his wife of 'worshipping that oul hat'. It had been a rough encounter, for they did not often argue. 'If you'd spend your time on a couple of budgies it would make all the difference. *At least a body could see a budgie and hear it sing.*' In the argument the budgies came off second best.

He nodded without enthusiasm at another mourner heading for the funeral. Beside him was a man in a cap. 'Mac's could do with a bit of a brush up,' he said in a low voice.

'Everything Mac puts on could do with a good brush up,' George said. 'Did you ever think of selling that hat?'

'Selling it?' Joey echoed, trying to keep his voice calm. 'Outright?' This was out of the blue.

'That's right. Outright.'

'Might do, George. One day.' George wasn't exactly the buyer he had in mind.

'I don't suppose you'd have a price in your thoughts?' George prompted.

'It would all depend, George.'

227

'Look Joey. You know bowlers inside out. I know you wouldn't be asking the moon. I know it's a good article. I just thought it would make a nice wedding present for the daughter's husband-to-be. She's to be married in a couple of weeks.'

Joey nodded. 'I don't think so.' There was no future in this conversation. All those Twelfths; all those years of cleaning; and his hat, his treasure, finishing up as a £20 wedding present, hardly worth looking after, probably a wee lad's toy.

No, it was worth a lot more. 'Look, George,' he said. 'I'll look around for something and let you know. Thanks for your interest.' He fixed it more firmly on his head.

The next moment they were swallowed up in a group of mourners.

When a Woman Shops

Women rarely shop in silence. It is a fairly safe assumption that a comparison between the comments made by a swarm of Belfast shoppers and those of a group in Manchester, Cardiff, Glasgow or Middlesborough would not leave Belfast in the ha'penny place.

> **I'm** dyin about this dress. Blue's my colour. The only thing is it fits me too soon. **"**

> **She** told me when she's down in the dumps she always gets herself a new hat and I said I often wondered where she got them. **"**

> **My** man's very thoughtful. He always washes his hands before he comes to bed. You couldn't say that of a lot of them. **"**

'I was in this shap in Ballyclare yesterday and I was countin my change. The oul shapkeeper lucked at me, an he says, "Can ye no count or can ye count none?" They're a funny lot down there.'

'Woman dear but that's serious weather we're gettin, isn't it?'

'Rain! Nobody could say that was rain. Sure there's hardly enough to cover a lafe.'

231

I saw that the woman in front of me in the supermarket would have a pay slip as long as a fat man's pair of braces so we moved till anor check point. You havta play with the head.

I didn't get over the door all day yesterday the way my corns was leppin.

I asked the girl for half a yard of red ribbon and said to mind she didn't cut the finger off herself. She give me a quare look.

'It was terrible in Majorca. Everything I put on stuck to me. My feet were burnt aff me.'

'No matter what style I get, as soon as I open my mouth you'd know where I came from.'

'I nivver like to ring him up for he's awful hard to life.'

234

They All Remember Andy

One of the consequences of getting long in the tooth is that things that once brought delight become sources of irritation. This doesn't just mean that you are no longer able to relish a lollipop or go tree-climbing.

Take the case of Andy, the Belfast Ormeau character of the twenties, lively memories of whom have flooded in to me from Ormeau Road veterans now living as far apart as Kent and Caledon, to say nothing of Birmingham and Clitheroe.

Andy's chief characteristics were a capacity for drink and a talent for irritating the law. He had a record of more than two hundred convictions for drunkenness.

Yet the former Ormeau Road citizens now scattered far and wide remember Andy with affection and associate him warmly with the happy days of their childhood. Mention of his name brings back those joyful boyhood years when legless Andy was the butt of their mockery, their parents' bidding ignored. Many of the latter spend hours jeering at Andy — but when their children were involved it was a different story.

Every area in the country must have the equivalent of Andy. As is the case with most down-and-outs, his background was a mystery. Some said he was driven to drink by a cruel father, others that his father had been too good to him.

Certainly his career as a 'character' was a lengthy one. To

run up such a toll of court convictions, besides the appearances when he would be allowed off with a fine, took a fair period of time.

It made an Ormeau youngster's day when Andy would stagger into their ken and the exchanges could begin.

Some days the youngsters would start the ball rolling by shouting, 'Come on, Andy. Chase the peelers.' Andy, it is reported, would roar back, 'Get away from me, ye wee ruffians. Get back to yer ma's apron.'

Letters recalling Andy and the happy memories cherished of him poured into me for weeks. One correspondent suggested that the man merited a statue.

There are suggestions that he was a boxer because of the shape of his nose, although it is more likely that this was the result of one of his contests with the police than a professional encounter in the ring.

The police must have been relieved to see the last of him, the arrival of the day when drink wasn't enough to send him thrashing and roaring through the streets looking for a fight. The one place where there was regret was among the staff of the prison canteen; apparently he was a first-class cook.

Usually it took six to ten policemen to control him when he was at his worst. Once four officers started to move him to the barracks in Donegall Pass, half a mile from the spot where he was causing trouble. After an hour they had covered only a few hundred yards.

Even the calling of a Black Maria was of no avail until someone had a brainwave. There was an undertaker's nearby which had a large sliding entrance door. Andy was pushed inside and the door pulled closed. The vehicle was then reversed to the door, which was quickly opened. 'Freedom,' thought Andy, and made a dash, only to find himself locked in the arms of the Black Maria.

Strange indeed that the luckless Andy should be recalled

by so many people (except maybe policemen) with such warmth, while those whose contribution to Ormeau was much more worthy are completely forgotten.

Agony Column of The Ballyragee Gazette

Ballyragee Gazette, Saturday, April 20

Sir, Can nathin be done about the milk packets? Me an my man spill the half of the milk before we can get one open. I hadda stap my husband from usin the hatchet on one yesterday. He was jumpin mad, an I wussent far behine him. Even the Black an Decker didden do the job. If nathin's goin till be done we're goin back till the battle next week.

Ballyragee Gazette, Saturday, May 28

Sir, We have a wee lad next door who's turnin intil a right wee nosey. I hope this letter will get something done about him. I don't know if his ma puts him up to it. He gets her steps and puts them up agin our fence. Then he sits and stares intil ar garden for all he's worth. He does nathin but stare. I keep wonderin what he expecks. I wonder is he hopin I'll cut his throat, because I might.

Ballyragee Gazette, Saturday, July 10

Sir, My son's mad about his flute ban. I doan mine that but he's started to bring them home at night to practise. They take over his bedroom, about eight of them, an start blowin, imaginin themselves to be eight Jimmy Galways. One of these days they'll crack the roof an the neighbours'll complain. How do you handle a neighbour who asts you to get the flutes stuffed? What do you stuff them with?

Ballyragee Gazette, Saturday, June 11

Sir, The orr day I was feelin terrible peckey an thought to myself after readin the death notices in the paper, 'Them that goes quick don't know they're livin.' See me? I'm thankful every day I doan fine anor fackulty gone. I was at the health centre an ast the nurse to make sure I gat an extra dose of tablets because last week the battle was half empey. All she give me was a glare when I toul her. You'd take your end at some people these days.

Ballyragee Gazette, Saturday, September 5

Sir, Please excuse paper. The wee lad's da made paper airplanes with what wus left of our note paper and all a cud get me hauns on wus the chile's exercise jatter. Cud ye tell me why it's so hard to get a stamp these days? It's nathin but a waste of a body's time tryin to get one at night. The man across the street from us collects them and he has hundreds, his wife says, but ast him for a 12p one an ye getta luck. Yu'd think he wud hev one he cud sell you to post a letter. What does the man collect them fer? Justa stick in an oul book?

Ballyragee Gazette, Saturday, November 15

Sir, I'm pleading with you to help me about my husband. He isn't a bad soul. He never bates me round the house. But he keeps goin till the big fights an it's terrible what this does till him. He comes home from them hoarse as a horse, sayin he has lost his voice because he was cheerin the fella that gat hammered. He always seems to cheer the one who gets knacked out. Even if he is hoarse he keeps sayin in his sleep, 'Hit him. Use yer elbow. Ye hev it in ye to make that mouse under his left eye into a bloody big rat. Have a go at the blirt.' He goes on for hours. Is there a ramedy for this?

Ballyragee Gazette, Saturday, December 20

Sir, I married a shoemaker. We have eight sons and a daughter. He mends all their shoes. I onny wonder shud I hev married a windey cleaner?

Such Good Neighbours

'We've always been awful good neighbours,' Mrs McQuish said. 'Close, I would even say. Well, till a while ago. I'd give her my recipes and she'd give me hers. A right wee woman. Couldn't do enough for you when you're in trouble. I've known her and her man for a good wheen of years now. She can make the most of herself. I'll say that.

'What gets me is that she likes to put on airs. She has a lovely fireplace in her front room but to my mind it's a bit fancy for a wee house like theirs. Sticks out like a sore thumb. You could see the Number 4 on their door if you had on a pair of dark glasses on a foggy night. That's the kine of woman she is.

'Don't think I'm being critical, mind you. Not one bit. I know she had a video before we did but that didn't bother me. She was welcome to it.

'Right enough her man couldn't do enough for her. Bought her a silver teapot for their anniversary and it was round the street in seconds. Mind you I had my doubts about that teapot. Maybe it was silver, maybe it wasn't. Looked to me like as if it fell aff a larry.

'Hear her talk sometimes an she gets on as if she'd been educated. Educated! Latta nansense. She was at the health clinic one day for an injection and told the doctor, "Give me a double dunt for I wasn't able to come last week."

'Hanest, she has an accent you could shake a stick at

243

when she's not thinkin. The pair of them get on as if they own the place. Lord and Lady Muck from Clabber Hill wouldn't be in it. It's the God's truth.

'Just because her man's eyebrows meet he always says it gives him an air. It's what she told me. Did you ever hear the like? The man's as common as dirt, so he is. He may be handy about the house — and when it comes to that he could see my man far enough — but puttin up a shelf isn't everything. There's more to life than a shelf.

'See her? She has a heart of corn if she would only let herself go. I'm not sure if it's her or her husband who's to blame. The way I see it I'd put all the blame on the same woman. Her Sammy would be alright if he was left alone.

'An there they are livin four houses from us and we haven't spoken for three years. Not since that night we looked in on them and we were havin a cup in our hauns. My man said as a joke, "An how many yards are you from the corner, Sammy? Sixteen? Eighteen? More?"

'"What are you talking about?" Sammy said.

'"Ach, man dear," my man said. "Saturday night there. You were at the bowling dinner, no doubt. Remember? It was about three in the morning. I asked you if I could give you a hand. 'Go to hell,' you told me, so I went on. You were busy anyway measurin the walls. Man you were doin the quare job."

'"He wasn't doing any such thing," says she, all indignant. "Sammy would never get into a state like that. Sammy wasn't measuring any walls."

'"You could have fooled me," says my husband. "For goodness' sake, Sammy, you were stoned out of your mind. No harm in that."

'"I'd rather nothing more was said about it," says yer woman.

'"Anyway I only intended it as a joke. No harm done," my man said.

'But here she is to us when we were goin: "It isn't a very nice thing to be insulted under your own roof."

'"Pity you spoke," I said till him afterwards. "Great pity."

'"It was nathin but a joke," says he. "I didn't intend any harm. The man was legless."

'Anyway it was only an excuse as far as she's concerned. I know rightly. It all goes back to the time my man wouldn't go guarantor for hers when he wanted to buy that Minor. He never forgive us. And nire does she. Anyway a woman whose bed's like Paddy's market at six o'clock at night can't be up to much. You can't get away from that.'

What Your Stars Are Saying

Most Ulster people put considerable faith in their stars. Few would be happy if they missed their horoscope. They will follow it even more faithfully if they are assessed in their own speech. 'I'm goin back till bed' indicates a poor day ahead. 'Mine's clinkin' shows that the stars are in your favour. 'It's like seein what yer tea cup tells ye — natta bitta harm in it' is the generally accepted view.

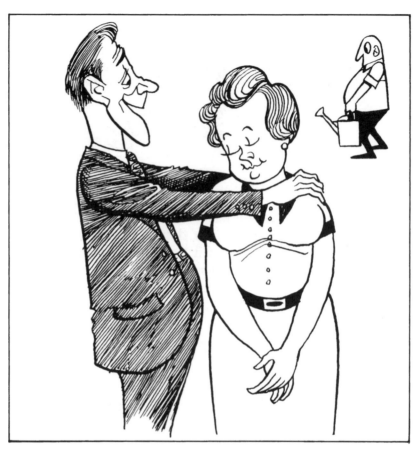

Aquarius
Jan 21 - Feb 19

CALL HER A WEE DOTE

This is a period when you should speak more affectionately to your wife. It won't do a bitta harm when she's been to the hairdresser's to say, 'Yew luck awful nice.' You'll find it will pay divvies. Man dear, just think what the wee woman does for ye, workin her fingers to the bone.

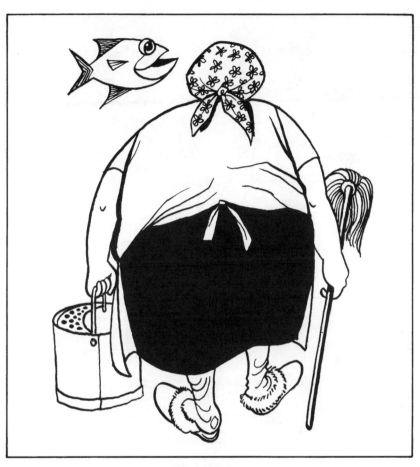

Pisces
Feb 20 - Mar 20

TIME FOR REDDIN UP

Git out the brush an map. It's tidying up time. Tho out all the junk you can get yer hauns on (just watch your man isn't among it). The things you'll nivver need again onny clutter up the house.

Aries

Mar 21 - Apr 20

GIVE UP THE PAN

You will be meeting someone who will knock you aff yer feet. Watch out, for you've bumped into people like that before an it didden do ye a bit of good. Men should tell their wives, 'I'm sick, sore and tired of the pan' an the cheers will raise the roof.

Taurus

Apr 21 - May 21

HAIR OF THE DOG

You'd be a wise man to ease aff the hair of the dog. Don't always suspeck people who give you advice. Just because you're musical doesn't mean you should think you're above everybody and go roun like death warmed up.

Gemini
May 22 - June 21

EASE AFF ON LETTIN ON

It's a lat better to have your frens saying you're dead nice than call you a big-head. You're too fond of goin at things like a bull at a gate but when you don't you're alright. Blue may be your lucky colour but don't put *all* your money on Linfeel.

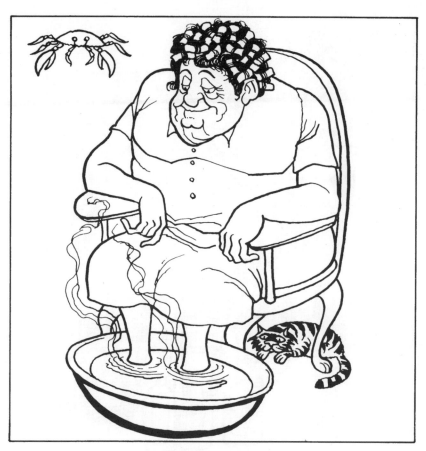

Cancer

June 22 - July 21

A SLAP IN THE EYE

Give your feet a right good steepin for you cud be futtin it the quare bit before long. This is no time of the year for hirplin. Expect a bit of a surprise at home. It could come from either himself or herself, and cud give ye a right dunt up the couter.

Leo

July 22 - Aug 22

A QUARE SHOCK

It's wrong to get the notion that a good supply of drink in the house will always get you by. You aren't all that better than the next fella. You'll win more frens if you don't let people think you're a bumptious oul skite.

Virgo
Aug 23 - Sep 23

JUST IGNORE THEMMUNS

You'll do remarkable if you cure yerself of bein an onion. Everybody likes you because you don't keep thinkin of yerself every minnit of the day. Just you stay the way you are.

Libra

Sep 24 - Oct 23

DON'T ACT THE GULPIN

If travellin anywhere make sure of the time for you're not much use in a hassle. Gettin intil a panic does nobody a bit of good. Besides, there's no sense in gettin yerself known as a big softy.

Scorpio
Oct 24 - Nov 21

BUY THE WIFE FLIRES

A good time to buy a car. The stars are in your favour if you
don't let the dealer take you in. Also a good time to buy your
wife flires, or take her out for a surprise supper.

Sagittarius
Nov 22 - Dec 20

STAP TH' GULDERIN

Far too often Sagittarians get their friends' backs up by
bawlin their heads aff at them. There's no call to raise your
voice. People will lissen if you speak softly. Just mine the
Ruby Murray song.

Capricorn
Dec 21 - Jan 20
YOU COULD BE SKINT

Don't go up the walls if you win a bit on the pools. That's the kine of money that nivver lasts. In one ear and out the other. Mine the days when you were short of the readies an nobody wud len ye a bean.

My Stummick's Churnin

He was happy with his patient and the good relationship they had established. Mrs Gourley was in her sixties and had varicose veins. He was from the East and while his medical knowledge was growing in assurance there were times when his patients had him guessing. Understanding clearly what they had to say was an important element in healing, he felt.

He put away his stethoscope and closed his bag. 'I'll see you again next weekend. You're coming along like a blazing house.' The phrase was one he had discovered a few days before and he was surprised at her blank look, he decided.

'Doctor, when you're going out the door,' said Mrs Gourley, pulling the blankets round her shoulders, 'Would you ask my daughter if she would bring me a jar?'

'Certainly.' He hurried out, his mind on his next patient, a gallstones victim who smoked thirty cigarettes a day, all high-tar.

At the bottom of the stairs Mrs Gourley's daughter was waiting, and he told her, 'Your mother's doing fine. She would like you to take her up a Scotch.'

'A Scotch, doctor?'

'That's what she said. She told me to tell you she would like a jar.'

'Don't be daft, man. She's cold. All she wants is a hot

260

water bottle. If I took her a Scotch she'd have a fit.'

'Sorry,' he said hastily and hurried away. It was yet another item to add to his list of localisms that spelt danger.

This included one expression that had set him off on his voyage into the vernacular when a woman patient told him, 'I'm not at myself.' Another lady had summed up her complaints with, 'My stummick's churnin.'

He had had some difficulty in coping with the request, 'Doctor, for God's sake could you take me out of myself?' In such cases his usual ploy was to ask, 'Could I have a few more details?' This helped to make it clear on another occasion that the woman who told him, 'My man's bad' did not mean her husband was a pillar of wickedness.

One early pitfall he had encountered came in the statement, 'My guts is up the pole.' It was a condition which, fortunately, did not call for a heart transplant.

The lady who insisted that she'd 'hadda discharge' was another early find. He had had a feeling of triumph in assuming she'd been made redundant.

'I can keep nothing down' and 'Everything keeps coming back' were other treasures of his bedside glossary. Noted less for their ambiguity than for their style were the statement, 'It's my legs, doctor. They're giving me gippo. What's the right time?' and the request, 'Could you do something about my husband? He keeps talking like he has a bit in his mouth.'

Another unexpected moment came when a patient asked, 'Could you hold my teeth till you examine my chest? For God's sake don't drap them for we're going to communion on Sunday.'

She was classed with the woman whose request was for another bottle of the medicine he had prescribed. 'You remember it?' she said, 'It was the colour of a ginger snap dipped in tea.'

'I know it,' he said cheerfully, thinking to himself, 'It's like hacking your way through a wood.'

Small Ads

Few things give away a community's life style or its general range of interests like the small advertisements placed in the local shop. They can betray the advertiser's religious beliefs, state of health, age group, social class, politics, hobbies, profession, even his financial standing. In each case that follows the spelling has been corrected.

The examples given are not intended to attract answers from interested parties; telephone numbers are therefore not included.

```
3 DOZ. UNCRACKED MILK BOTTLES

TOP CONDITION.
£30 the lot O.N.O.

EXCEPTIONAL OPPORTUNITY
```

<u>GOING FOR A SONG:</u>
SET of HOLIDAY POSTCARDS, mainly
from Spain. (Two from Corsica,
three from Isle of MAN) Stamps
removed

Twin Buggy, double cover
Changeable from Union Jack to
Tricolour.Can also be altered
to ALL BLACK, showing neutral.

Needs slight repair.

<u>£25</u> O.N.O.

Andersonstown district

Ballymena postman has
25 pairs non-matching socks
on offer. All Christmas presents

NO REASONABLE OFFER

REFUSED!!

FORTY POTS OF MARMALADE

gone slightly off. Happened
only last week. Could be of
value for compost heap.
NO REASONABLE OFFER REFUSED.
Ballygomartin Road area

FOR SALE

Collection of Rock Records. Only 4 un-
cracked. Bargain at

£1 o.n.o.

Cromac St. district

for sale:

set of golf clubs, all but 3 in prime
condition. Were smashed by owner after
throwing away Cup Final match when 4 up.

Bag has Co. Down badge

for sale

3 one-legged pairs trousers.
Excellent material. Tailor made.

Queen's Rag Night relic

CHEAP for quick sale

LOST!

Siamese cat answering to name of

BALLYBEFOREYE

Lost in Greenisland area. Well-
behaved but doesn't like horses
or fish.All white

REWARD OFFERED!

FOR SALE

Quantity of broken slates.Could be of use

to D.I.Y. enthusiast.Delivery taken care of.

QUID the lot O.N.O.

(Sandy Row district)

FOR SALE

        12 horse-shoes for decorative
purposes. In prime condition. At £10
a real giveaway. Reason for sale -
owner bankrupt.

                    (Snugville St. area)

For sale!

    Walking Stick. bears initials
G.H.T.V.E. Has covered 1,000 miles
but has big mileage left
Family heirloom.

            Malone Road area

<u>BOWLER HAT</u>

As new. Looked after. size 7½.

Used for fourteen Twelfths, six

funerals and three weddings.

            £15 O.N.O

(Antrim Road locality)

Wake Etiquette

Anyone invited to a wake for the first time should remember that it differs considerably from any other gathering of mourners. It should be taken for granted that the corpse, whether covered or not, is often addressed as if he was present in person.

For example, when invited to 'drink the health' of the deceased the convention is to gesture towards the coffin and say with heartiness, 'Your very good health!'

Similarly, there is nothing unusual about it if one of the guests says to the corpse, 'Your wife was tellin me that the day before you passed away she bought you a pair of long johns an the next day it was so bitter cold she was sure you would have felt the good of them and put them on you. She did right, now, didn't she?' The mourners will think nothing of waiting fractionally as if expecting confirmation from the deceased.

Nothing transforms a person's character like a wake. The greatest villain unhung will be made to resemble a paragon of virtue.

'He was a giant of a man in this townland' is sure to win murmurs of approval, besides a quick response to the speaker's signal that his glass is empty.

A wake newcomer would be well advised to go into training. It is no place for a man who cannot hold his drink. The drinking, the revelry, the crack, the stories have been known to last well beyond six a.m.

Confusion can sometimes arise, for anything can happen. During the revelry at John McDade's wake it was discovered that so many people had been sitting on the edge of the bed on which he was laid out that it had collapsed. The chief mourners rose to the occasion by deciding to prop the corpse on three chairs until the undertaker arrived. One of them called to guests below, 'Three chairs for John McDade.' Instantly came the response, 'All together, boys. Three cheers for John. Hip, hip . . . .'

As the night progresses the women tend to drift away. Inevitably in the early hours 'men's talk' takes over. The question will even be asked when the audience is all male, 'What on earth did he ever see in that string of misery of his? Dammit, his death rattle had hardly died away before she had a notice stuck on the door, "House Private". But then, of course, he wasn't a man to ever expect the worst. Only last week there he got a bad hair cut and when he told me about it he said, "Ach it isn't as terrible as a short leg. Sure it'll grow again."'

A sense of humour can be extended beyond the grave, as happened at one big Tyrone wake. The story was told of the deceased that shortly after buying a brace of prize cockerels he had had to see the doctor about a pain in his leg. 'I don't suppose it could be crowing pains, doctor?' he had asked with a grin. The mourners heartily agreed that 'He could crack a joke with the best of them.'

At another farewell one woman, taking a cautious sip of her drink, said, 'My man went up to see him an kem back with the word that he'd be under boord before night. The next night I was in bed when my man came in to tell me the poor soul had got a seizure. I might as well have got up, it was such a shock.'

It can be said of a wake that at least it provides an opportunity to commune with the dead. This happened on one occasion when the deceased was told through his coffin,

271

'I'll never forget the night we had last Christmas there. God but you were goin well, an herself nivver heard a word about it. There you were stannin on the bar-room counter singing Danny Boy. It nearly brought the roof down. Ye could have been on TV. D'ye mind the night? Ye must mind it.'

There was general agreement that the night must indeed have been a memorable one.

Belfast for Aliens

Attendants in the leisure centres are invariably caring and attentive. Occasionally they'll look at you as if wondering 'What on earth are you doing here?'

Banks treat the public with complete disdain at lunch time. They are then rigidly closed. You must keep your cash in your pocket. It's no go if you want to cash a cheque.

Barmen usually disgruntled. Give the impression of being grossly under-tipped.

Not terribly talkative. Safest subject to mention is Barry McGuigan.

Black taxis are plentiful but the other passengers are usually resentful of the stranger. The driver's only contribution to any conversation is 'Where till?'

Bookshops are of a good standard but there should be more of them. Those in existence are too far apart.

City buses should not be expected to provide the last word in comfort. A large number have un-upholstered seats. Drivers keep their distance.

Good cup of coffee not easily to be had. Standards vary tremendously. Best bet is to try a café with harassed looking waitress with dirty finger-nails.

Hamburgers sold from vans superior to those elsewhere. Much better value and service on a higher scale.

Ice cream standard appallingly low but starting to get better. Take-away packs not worth buying, as a rule.

Nurses are nearly always in good spirits. They enjoy being chatted up in a light-hearted way. Often are victims of over-zealous discipline.

Pedestrian zones are used too extensively by motorists. Walkers are treated by drivers as if they shouldn't be alive.

Place to go for the Marks and Spencer store with the biggest cash turnover of any in Britain. Southern accents of the shoppers may give the idea you're not in Belfast. These are Dublin bargain hunters who come up in droves because the prices are lower in the North.

Police officers are generally friendly and helpful. They'll chat affably but always underneath will show caution which they aren't going to throw to the wind.

Public toilet attendants constantly wear a disgruntled look. They give the impression that they have just discovered a pools coupon they forgot to post which would have won them £50,000.

Street wear not a patch on English cities. Women's fashion shops don't reflect what is worn outside. Prices high. Men dress with indifference.

Supermarkets are uncomfortable for shopping. Not enough space for shoppers. Rush hour parking arrangements are maddening.

Traffic wardens are as sharp and efficient as they come. They carry an air of having heard your excuse many times before and they're getting weary of it.

Unkempt gardens are in the minority compared with those tended with loving care. Some suburban houses are a paradise of colour.